Nikki Riggsbee

Irish
Wolf[hound]

Everythin[g] [about] [P]urchase,
Care, Nutrition, Behavior,
and Training

Filled with Full-color Photographs
Illustrations by Michele Earle-Bridges

BARRON'S

CONTENTS

INTRODUCING THE IRISH WOLFHOUND

"I will give thee a dog which I got in Ireland. He is huge of limb, and for a follower equal to an able man. Moreover, he hath a man's wit and will bark at thine enemies but never at thy friends. And he will see by each man's face whether he be ill or well disposed to thee. And he will lay down his life for thee."
From the Icelandic Saga of Nial

Description

The Irish Wolfhound is the tallest and largest galloping hound, the tallest American Kennel Club (AKC) breed, and probably the tallest breed of dog in the world today.

A rough-coated Greyhound-type dog, the Irish Wolfhound is classified as a sighthound that hunts visually rather than by scent. The Wolfhound is strong and graceful, tall but not bulky. It is an ancient breed, identified in art and writing over 2,000 years ago. The official dog of Ireland, the Irish Wolfhound hunted wolf, Irish elk, and other large game. Hunting singly or in pairs rather than in a pack, they

The most obvious characteristic of an Irish Wolfhound is his great size.

were fast enough to catch the prey and strong enough to dispatch it.

The paradox of the Irish Wolfhound is that it has both power and speed. Great size and strength give power but reduce speed. The fastest body style for speed lacks power. The successful balance of the Irish Wolfhound provides both.

Coat and Color

Along with his great size and Greyhound-like shape, the Irish Wolfhound's coat is a defining characteristic. The rough coat suits the harsh and capricious climate of Ireland. It is coarse and wiry, especially long above the eyes and under the jaw, forming the characteristic eyebrows and beard. It is a double coat, with the

TIP

Coat Color Can Change

Wheaten and red can change color over the life of the dog, becoming lighter or darker or even gray. The amount of brindling or stripes can vary over the life of the dog. When born, the black predominates, and the newborn is quite dark. The black fades as the puppy grows, and more of the lighter base coat is seen. Then as the adult Wolfhound ages, each year the dog looks darker again.

outer coat longer and rough and the undercoat shorter and dense. It is the undercoat that is shed.

Wolfhounds come in many colors. Gray is the most common, but coats can be other solid colors, including white, wheaten (tan), fawn (reddish tan), red, or black. They can also be brindle, with black stripes in a chevron pattern across the solid base color. There is no preferred color; do not buy a "valuable and rare" colored Wolfhound.

A nonwhite Irish Wolfhound may have white markings on his chest, toes, feet, and the tip of his tail. A Wolfhound can have a dilute gene that produces a blue coat color, with liver-colored nose and lips. These are considered faults on show dogs, but as long as the dog is healthy and has a good temperament, they don't affect a dog's value as a pet.

Today's Wolfhound

Today the typical Irish Wolfhound spends more time on the couch than hunting. Called "Gentle Giants," they are treasured companions and beloved members of the family.

Irish Wolfhounds are great pets for suitable homes that want a giant dog with a laid back temperament. They are friendly, gentle, and good with children. They enjoy living with other dogs. Most Wolfhounds today can be found on the bed taking a nap, taking a walk with their owners, sharing the couch, or just hanging out with a member of the family.

Note the differences in size and appearance of the various sighthounds. From the left: Irish Wolfhound, Scottish Deerhound, Borzoi, Greyhound, Afghan Hound, Saluki, Whippet, and Basenji.

Like all sighthounds, Irish Wolfhounds were developed to chase down prey and therefore are capable of great speed for their size.

Typical Weight and Height Values

Age (months)	Weight (pounds [kg])		Height (inches [cm])	
	male	female	male	female
birth	1–2 (0.5–1)	1–2 (0.5–1)	—	—
2	22–30 (10–14)	18–25 (8–11)	18–21 (46–53)	18–21 (46–53)
6	80–100 (36–45)	75–95 (34–43)	27–32 (64–81)	26–30 (66–76)
12	105–134 (47–60)	100–117 (45–53)	29–34 (74–86)	28–32 (71–81)
24	125–150 (56–68)	110–129 (50–58)	30–35 (76–89)	29–33 (74–84)
36	135–175 (61–79)	115–150 (52–68)	30–36 (76–91)	29–34 (74–86)

Note: This chart shows typical sizes at different ages. Your own Wolfhound might vary substantially from these numbers.

How Big Do They Get?

Very big!

The AKC standard description of the breed calls for adult males to be at least 32 inches (81 cm) tall (measured from the top of the shoulder blades to the ground) and weigh 130 pounds (58 kg). Adult females should be at least 30 inches (79 cm) tall and weigh 120 pounds (54 kg). These minimums apply to show dogs, but many fully mature Wolfhounds exceed them. Males often average 33–36 inches (84–91 cm) in height and weigh

Irish Wolfhounds would often work in pairs when hunting wolves.

between 135 and 175 pounds (61 and 79 kg). Females may range from 31 to 34 inches (79 to 86 kg) tall and from 115 to 150 pounds (52 to 68 kg). There is a great variation in sizes among adult Wolfhounds, but even at smaller sizes, they are taller than other dogs and very impressive.

To get so big, Irish Wolfhounds grow very quickly. Such rapid growth stresses puppies physically, especially their bones and joints. The fast-growing Wolfhound puppies must be fed properly. Inappropriate exercise by developing puppies can cause problems. See the chapter "Caring for and Feeding Your Irish Wolfhound" for how to raise your growing Wolfhound.

Puppies sleep a lot; it is exhausting to grow so fast. Long naps have a nice side benefit in housebreaking. Puppies don't need to relieve themselves while asleep and so don't need to go out to potty as often. Because they are so big so young, their larger capacity for holding it means that they needn't be taken out as often as smaller dogs.

Even though Wolfhound puppies are bigger than most adults of other breeds, they are physically, mentally, emotionally, and behaviorally still puppies. They will be awkward and constantly adjusting to their continuously changing size. They will learn quickly but have a short attention span. They will zoom, bounce, jump, and misbehave, as any puppy will. Remember to adjust your expectations to your puppy's age, not size.

Irish Wolfhounds get close to their adult height by the time they are 12 to 15 months old. At that age, they are gangly adolescents. They fill out and mature over the next year or two. As a member of a giant breed, the Irish Wolfhound is not fully mature until about three years of age.

You can tell if a dog is still growing taller by checking the growth plates, most easily found at the pastern joint (ankle) of his front legs. Bones grow at both ends. When the growth plates are producing new bone, you can see and feel a bump at the pastern joint. When the bone has reached its full length, the growth plate will close, and there will no longer be a bump. At that time, your Wolfhound will have most of his height. This bump is perfectly normal and more pronounced in a giant breed than in smaller breeds. People less familiar with giant breeds may think that the dog's large and lumpy pastern joints are a deformity, but now you know better.

History

Descended from the mighty Cu, the giant rough-coated Greyhound-style dog of early Ireland, the Irish Wolfhound was known in pre-Christian times. They were found in Europe wherever the Celtic people went. When the Celts invaded Rome, they brought their dogs. In 391 A.D, the first recorded reference to the breed was made by the Roman Consul Quintus Aurelius, referring to a "gift of seven Irish dogs." They were also brought back to Rome when the Romans invaded the British Isles and were included in the Roman shows and games.

Called the "Irish Wolfdog" and "Irish Greyhound" in ancient times, the Wolfhounds went to war with their masters, in addition to hunting large game and guarding their owners' possessions. The Celts settled in Ireland around the sixth century B.C., bringing their giant hounds with them. Irish legends and myths contain multiple references to the prowess of the Wolfhounds and the high esteem accorded them.

One is the legend of Chulainn, a famous Irish hero. He came to the castle of a king, but a huge hound protected the entrance. He fought with the dog all day and night before he was able to slay it and enter the castle. The king was despondent at the loss of the dog that he had left to guard his possessions. Chulainn was so remorseful at having killed so great a hound that he offered to be the king's hound for a year. He became known at that point as CuChulainn, the "Hound of Cullain."

Only kings and noblemen were allowed to own Irish Wolfhounds, the number allowed commensurate with the owner's position. They were also given as gifts to important guests and visiting royalty. Eventually, too many Irish hounds were leaving the country as gifts to foreign kings and princes. Oliver Cromwell halted this practice in 1652 with a law banning the export of Wolfhounds.

By the seventeenth century, much of the large game was gone, and the Irish wolf and elk were extinct. Without an important job to do and with poor economic times and a famine in Ireland, the Wolfhound nearly died out.

Fortunately, Captain George Augustus Graham became intrigued by the breed and was determined to rescue it from extinction. Graham, born

Even after many centuries, the link between Irish Wolfhounds and Irish culture remains strong. Here a "Gentle Giant" enjoys the company of two young step dancers.

Irish Wolfhounds offer a giant welcome to friendly visitors.

in Scotland, was initially interested in the Scottish Deerhound, which is believed to be derived from the early Irish Wolfdog when the Irish invaded Scotland with their dogs. Beginning in 1862, Graham gathered as many of the existing Irish Wolfhounds as he could that traced their blood to the hounds of old. Using these few dogs and judicious outcrosses to the related Scottish Deerhound and to Borzoi, Tibetan Mastiff, and Great Dane, the breed was revived in the form resembling the ancient hounds.

Graham's goal was not only to save the breed but also to have the Wolfhound resemble the magnificent ancient Cu, with great size, power, majesty, and speed. The results were

accepted as a revival of the breed, and in 1879, the Irish Kennel Club dog show included the Irish Wolfhound.

Temperament

One of the most endearing characteristics of Irish Wolfhounds is their temperament. They are calm, gentle companions, and laid-back members of the family. After a lively puppyhood and a moderate amount of daily exercise, they are quite content to keep quiet company with you.

They are loving dogs with a great capacity for friendship with people and other dogs. They are not one-person dogs. They need to live in the house with their family, not be banished to the yard or a kennel.

They are intelligent and quite able to learn what is requested of them. Remember, however, that sighthounds are independent hunters and thinkers who work at great distances from people. They don't wait for detailed commands from their owners to hunt and slay the wolf. They wouldn't check back with their masters, asking, "What shall I do next?" If they did, they would never get the job done.

Wolfhounds are not watchdogs or guard dogs. They are not aggressive towards people, and aggression should never be encouraged, for it is foreign to the breed. Their size alone is sufficient deterrent against an unfriendly stranger. A Wolfhound owner tells of walking on her property with her dog and seeing a suspicious stranger walking outside her fence. The Wolfhound positioned himself between her and the stranger and stood his ground until the stranger was well away.

They are not gratuitous barkers, although they may occasionally bark when they perceive the need. Some are singers, though, and may throw back their heads and whoo-oo-oo-oo. In some groups of Wolfhounds, there may be a choirmaster who starts the song, and all the rest join in. You are welcome to sing along, of course.

Irish Wolfhounds are gentle with children. They are aware of their size and power and restrain it around those who are smaller and weaker. Most Wolfhounds enjoy living with other dogs, especially with other Wolfhounds or Deerhounds. They prefer being part of a group,

When they put their front paws on a person's shoulders, most Irish Wolfhounds are as tall or taller than the person they are facing.

Irish Wolfhound at a Glance

Listed below are some important traits you should consider when selecting a breed and how much of each trait you can expect in a Wolfhound.

	High	Moderate	Low
Size	✔		
Energy level			✔
Exercise needs		✔	
Friendliness	✔		
Playfulness		✔	
Overt affection level	✔		
Devotion to family	✔		
Watch dog ability			✔
Trainability		✔	
Grooming needs		✔	
Good with children	✔		
Good with other dogs	✔		

Testament to the Wolfhound

In 1770, Oliver Goldsmith described the Irish Wolfhound: "The last variety and most wonderful of all that I shall mention is the great Irish Wolfdog, that may be considered as the first of the canine species . . . bred up to the houses of the great . . . . Nevertheless he is extremely beautiful and majestic in appearance, being the greatest of the dog kind to be seen in the world."

Irish Wolfhound puppies are small for only a very short time.

with people and other dogs, to being alone. Some individual dogs have a strong prey drive, however, and when they are around small animals that run, that running may invoke the prey drive.

Dignity, sensitivity, and stoicism are characteristic of Irish Wolfhounds. As big as they are, they have soft temperaments. If they feel they are being treated roughly or unfairly, they will leave, mentally or physically. Therefore, they should never be harshly corrected. A gentle correction is sufficient for this giant.

Wolfhounds tolerate much discomfort and pain. They won't come tell you or complain when they are ill. It is incumbent on you as the owner to observe small changes in behavior that may signal that your dog has a medical or other problem.

The Irish Wolfhound has a characteristic temperament for the breed. But all dogs are individuals with many personal differences. Some are more energetic; others are less active. Some Wolfhounds are more introverted than others. Some Wolfhounds are mischievous or destructive, while others never get into trouble.

Each Irish Wolfhound is entitled to an owner who enjoys the typical Irish Wolfhound characteristics and who also cherishes the dog's unique personality and individuality. With this approach, your relationship with your Wolfhound should be successful and a mutually beneficial lifelong friendship.

Is an Irish Wolfhound the Right Dog for You?

Size is the biggest factor in determining if an Irish Wolfhound is right for you. This dog is as big as another person in your home. Make sure

An Irish Wolfhound with a Celtic cross, both symbols of a proud, ancient heritage.

you know what that means and that you want it before you get a Wolfhound.

Size Considerations

Your adult Wolfhound is taller than you are when you are sitting down. When he stands in front of the television, he not only blocks the screen entirely from your view, but the remote control won't work. He can investigate what is on any table or countertop; if food is there, he can help himself. Lying down, he takes up a lot of floor, couch, or bed space.

If you are only comfortable with a "House Beautiful" home, then an Irish Wolfhound is not for you. The knick-knacks will get knocked about if they are in the range of a wagging Wolfhound tail. Many Irish Wolfhounds, though, are very aware of their size and can navigate a room full of furniture and decorations and not touch anything.

An Irish Wolfhound may well be bigger, heavier, and stronger than you are. You will need to learn how to walk your Wolfhound on lead so that you are in control. The sighthound's instinct to run is very strong. When interested in something to chase, your Wolfhound won't hear you call. You must be able to keep the dog on lead at all times when outside in an unfenced area. If you want a dog that will stay nearby off lead, then a Wolfhound is not the dog for you.

Although you don't need acres, a good-sized backyard is handy as a place for the dog to relieve himself and for running a few times each day. You and your Wolfhound might enjoy neighborhood walks, but it can be a nuisance to walk several times a day in

inclement weather if your yard is inadequate or unfenced. A tall, sturdy, aboveground fence is needed for this giant.

When he moves his bowels, it won't be a tiny pile hidden in the grass, unless you have very tall grass. During your walks, you will need to clean up after your dog if you intend to remain on good terms with your neighbors. You must pick up after your dog in your own yard, too, to keep it from becoming a minefield.

Not all Wolfhounds chew, but those who do can destroy a good portion of a sofa or round off the corners of your dresser. In the yard, unsupervised, they may trim the foliage as high as they can reach, at least four feet off the ground. Wolfhounds can dig cavern-sized holes, large enough to contain the dog or a small lawn mower. Will you be able to deal with these situations with humor and persistence, and still love your Wolfhound?

While they take a lot of room, Wolfhounds are laid back and easy to live with.

A child can tell all her secrets to her Wolfhound.

Do you have transportation sized for a Wolfhound? If you have only a small car or no extra room, you'll have to upsize your vehicle to carry your Wolfhound. Your adult dog can easily take up the entire back seat.

Benefits of Great Size

Part of the joy of having a Wolfhound is admiring this giant. These dogs are awesome when they stand alert looking at something in the distance, the epitome of "great size and commanding appearance." The soft, gentle expression melts hearts. The power exhibited when they are galloping around the yard is exciting. Next to a Wolfhound, other dogs are . . . well . . . small.

You don't have to lean over to pet an Irish Wolfhound. If you somehow forget to pet him, he will lean on you (a canine version of a hug) or nudge your hand as a reminder.

The Irish Wolfhound's great size is a deterrent to unwelcome visitors. When a stranger rings the doorbell, you can take the dog with you to answer the door. A dog's head at about 4 feet (1.2 m) high looking out a front window will discourage most troublemakers from coming up to your house. Yet, because Wolfhounds are not aggressive dogs, visiting friends and children are not in danger.

You won't be anonymous on walks with your Wolfhound; they are people magnets. Most people who see you will come to meet your giant dog, pet him, and ask the same clever questions that you will get tired of hearing. "Who's walking whom?" "You should get a saddle for him." "I'll bet he eats you out of house and home." "How much does he weigh?" People whom you wouldn't want to meet, however, cross to the other side of the street, fearful of such a big dog.

Irish Wolfhounds are people magnets; you're bound to meet new people while walking your Wolfhound.

Everything They Do Is Big

Owning an Irish Wolfhound is a big responsibility. It is an expensive breed to purchase and maintain. You need not be wealthy, but you must be willing and able to buy what the dog needs. No Irish Wolfhound should be denied veterinary care because the owner cannot afford it. Giant breeds require larger doses, so medications and some procedures will cost more. The dog will need more of products given based on weight, such as heartworm preventative and flea control. Boarding a giant dog is more expensive. If your first questions are about costs or if you can't afford it, don't get the dog.

When Irish Wolfhounds make mistakes, they make big ones. During housebreaking, mistakes will take a roll of paper towels to clean up. On the other hand, they are incredibly easy to housebreak. Once they know the place they are supposed to go and can get there, there will be few accidents. Most Wolfhound owners report that their puppies can be housebroken by three or four months of age.

Wolfhounds are great with children of all ages. They are calm, gentle, and stoic. But remember that they have a great size and weight advantage over small children. Are you willing to supervise an active young and very big Wolfhound puppy that outweighs a child

Irish Wolfhounds enjoy traveling with their owners and meeting other dogs.

by two or three times? It is unfair to both the dog and the child if you don't manage the situation effectively.

Wolfhounds Are Moderate, Too

Irish Wolfhounds are low-energy dogs. They won't turn your house into a racetrack as more active smaller dogs may. A few laps around the yard or a daily walk or two will satisfy their need for exercise. They are undemanding dogs with a low work ethic; you needn't constantly think of activities to keep them busy and out of trouble.

The amount of food they eat is less than expected for their size. They may be three times as big as another dog and yet eat only twice as much.

Grooming

The Irish Wolfhound's rough natural looking coat needs regular attention, or it will mat and be dirty. Wolfhounds thrive as housedogs, so you must commit to a level of grooming so that the dog will be welcomed and pleasant to have in your home.

If groomed regularly, you will find Wolfhounds relatively clean dogs to have in the house. Brushed regularly, they don't shed hair all over the house, and the non-oily coat means minimal doggy odor and a cleaner dog.

Life Span

The biggest downside of Irish Wolfhounds is their shorter life span, 6.5 years on average. There is an inverse correlation between size

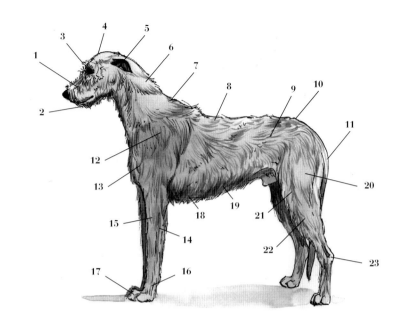

1. Muzzle
2. Beard
3. Eyebrows
4. Skull
5. Ears
6. Neck
7. Withers
8. Back
9. Loin
10. Croup
11. Tail
12. Shoulder
13. Upper arm
14. Elbow
15. Front leg
16. Pastern
17. Foot
18. Chest
19. Tuck up
20. Thigh
21. Stifle
22. Second thigh
23. Hock

External anatomy of the Irish Wolfhound.

and longevity: the larger the breed, the shorter the average life expectancy. A small compensating benefit is that you won't have years of geriatric problems. Every Wolfhound owner must be familiar with some health issues; see the chapter "Your Irish Wolfhound's Health."

Although some people choose not to have Wolfhounds because of their shorter life, it is a testament to the charm and endearing qualities of the breed that many people will always have Wolfhounds in spite of the fewer years.

Are You Right for Him?

Most Irish Wolfhounds that end up in the pound or in rescue are those acquired by people not prepared to deal with a giant dog.

They claim that the dog got too big, too hard to handle, or too expensive. You should visit as many homes with Wolfhounds as you can, meet the dogs, and talk to the owners.

Make certain that everyone in your household is enthusiastic about the getting a Wolfhound. If your spouse wants a small dog or your child is afraid of big dogs, don't get a Wolfhound, hoping they will eventually accept it.

Irish Wolfhounds are magnificent dogs, but they are not for everyone. If you and all the members of your household are eager to include this giant breed in your home and your life, then you can begin your search for your Wolfhound and your until-death-do-us-part commitment to the dog.

FINDING THE RIGHT IRISH WOLFHOUND

You've done your homework, visited some Irish Wolfhounds, and decided that this would be a great breed for you. But, Wal-Mart doesn't carry them, and they aren't listed in the yellow pages. So where will you find one?

Reputable Breeders

Reputable breeders are the best source for good Irish Wolfhound puppies. Most reputable breeders breed dogs as a hobby, not to make money, and are sometimes called hobby breeders. The goal of reputable breeders is to improve continuously the quality of the dogs they breed. They select the highest quality dogs that they can to breed and then keep the best of each litter to breed the next generation. The puppies that are not kept for breeding can be sold as pets.

Reputable breeders are experts in their breeds. They provide the best care for their dogs. They are familiar with problems that can occur in a breed and how to manage or correct

Reputable breeders are the best source for finding a quality Irish Wolfhound.

them, if possible. When you get a puppy from such a breeder, you have a resource for the life of your dog for information, answers to your questions, and help with problems.

Serious breeders are a safety net for the puppies they produce. If a puppy buyer cannot keep the dog at any age for any reason, serious breeders will take the dog back. They carefully screen prospective puppy homes to avoid this and to ensure that the puppies are in the best possible homes. But divorce, illness, or economic hardship may happen. If such an event prevents an owner from keeping the Wolfhound, the reputable breeder will want the dog to come back home.

Most serious breeders in the United States compete with their dogs in AKC conformation dog shows. The basic purpose of dog shows is to evaluate breeding stock. If enough judges

TIP

Irish Wolfhound Registration Statistics

In 2004, 980 Irish Wolfhound dogs were registered with the American Kennel Club, an increase of 60 dogs over the previous year. Wolfhound registration ranked 84th among the 151 AKC breeds. During the same year, 201 Irish Wolfhound litters were registered.

consider a dog to be superior to the other dogs competing, that dog becomes a champion.

Ideally, one or both of your puppy's parents will be champions. The next two generations (grandparents and great-grandparents) in the puppy's pedigree should include many champions. Dogs that are AKC champions will have the designation "Ch" in front of their names in the puppy's pedigree.

Some breeders compete with their Wolfhounds in performance events to confirm that their dogs are able to do what the breed was developed for. Lure coursing competition tests the original sight-hunting skills of the Wolfhound. You may find some dogs with lure coursing or other performance titles in your puppy's pedigree. Some AKC lure coursing title designations are JC, SC, MC, or LCX behind a dog's name or FC in front of his name. American Sighthound Field Association (ASFA) also holds competitions, and offers the titles of Field Champion (FCh) and several levels of Lure Courser of Merit (LCM). If you want to lure course with your puppy, seek breeders

who breed with that goal and a puppy whose ancestors have coursing titles.

See the chapter "Activities with Your Wolfhound" for more information on dog shows, lure coursing, and more.

Where Not to Get a Wolfhound

Don't look for a Wolfhound at flea markets, auctions, or from newspaper advertisements. Only commercial and backyard breeders sell dogs in this way; reputable breeders will not. Backyard breeders advertise their puppies in newspapers; reputable breeders don't have to.

Commercial breeders are sometimes called "puppy mills" because they produce so many puppies. Backyard breeders operate on a smaller scale, often selling puppies from their homes. But the primary interest of both is the same: to make money selling puppies. Occasional breeders are those who breed the family pet, sometimes for extra money and sometimes to show the children the miracle of birth.

These are not good sources of Wolfhound puppies because the dogs are usually lower quality and have more health and temperament problems than those from reputable hobby breeders. The care the dogs get is less. The people breeding are less knowledgeable.

Don't be taken in by the term "championship lines." It usually means that somewhere in the puppy's pedigree, many generations ago, there was a dog or two bred by a good breeder. It doesn't mean that the puppies or their parents are good quality.

Puppies labeled as "AKC" are not necessarily top quality. AKC puppies are those eligible to be registered with the American Kennel Club. The only requirement for a puppy to be registered with the AKC is that both parents are AKC registered. It doesn't warrant the quality of the parents or the puppy. Good quality Irish Wolfhound puppies will be eligible for AKC registration. But all AKC Irish Wolfhound puppies are not necessarily good quality. AKC registration is like getting a license plate for a car. It must be a car. But it could be a limousine or a jalopy.

How to Find a Reputable Irish Wolfhound Breeder

The two best places to find reputable Irish Wolfhound breeders are the Irish Wolfhound Club of America and at AKC dog shows.

Most serious breeders in the United States belong to the Irish Wolfhound Club of America (IWCA). The IWCA is the parent club of the breed, responsible for the breed within AKC. Breeders outside the United States usually belong to the national Irish Wolfhound club in their country.

The IWCA has an excellent web site for people who want to learn about Wolfhounds and to find breeders. It includes names of people to contact plus much information about Wolfhounds and is an excellent starting place for someone looking for a puppy.

The AKC web site is another resource for locating Irish Wolfhounds. It can identify dog clubs and breeder referral contacts in the state where you live.

You can find Wolfhound breeders and owners at most dog shows. Check AKC's web site to find the dates and locations of dog shows in your area. At these shows, you can meet the breeders themselves. You can also meet other people who own Wolfhounds who can tell you about the breeders from whom they got their dogs. Best of all, you can meet the dogs themselves.

The majority of reputable breeders actively participate in dog shows to earn championship titles on their dogs.

See "HOW-TO: Breeders on the Internet" for more information.

Finding a Breeder Is Not the Same as Finding a Litter

As you contact breeders, you will discover that they may not have puppies available. Responsible breeders usually don't breed often enough to have puppies regularly. One reason is that they want the best homes for their puppies, and they don't want to produce more puppies than they can place in good homes.

Healthy ten-day-old Irish Wolfhound puppies like these weigh about three to four pounds each.

Expect that you may have to wait for a litter to be born. Use the time to get to know the breeders, and let them get to know you and the home you will provide for one of their dogs. Find out when the breeder is planning a litter. Ask the breeder to consider you for a puppy from the next litter. Keep in touch with the breeders whose dogs you like. Good breeders get many inquiries. They will remember those people who learn about the breed, visit their dogs (if possible), and contact them periodically about the status of the upcoming litters.

Evaluating a Breeder

The breeder who lives closest to you or has the best web site, the most dogs, or the biggest kennel is not necessarily the best breeder. You are looking for a responsible breeder who will be your best source for getting a nice puppy, information, and support for the life of the Wolfhound. Talk to as many Wolfhound breeders as you can to find the one you like best and whose dogs you like best. Pick your breeder first, then get one of that breeder's puppies.

If at all possible, visit the breeder. Meet the breeder's family of dogs. They should be healthy looking and well maintained. The place where the dogs are kept should be clean and comfortable. Ideally, they should live in the house and be part of the family. They should have adequate room to run and play safely.

The dogs should have good temperaments. Most should come up to welcome you and enjoy being petted. All dogs are not extroverts, however; some may take a few minutes before they come up to you. Be suspicious of breeders who don't want you to meet their dogs.

When you meet Wolfhounds, remember that they are tall dogs; you needn't lean over them to pet them. The dogs will be more comfortable if you do not put your face in their face or hug them. In human terms, leaning over and hugging someone are affectionate gestures. But in dog body language, they are domineering actions. They don't know you yet, and both behaviors can be viewed as threatening by some dogs.

As the breeder's adult dogs look and act, so will your puppy probably look and act in a few years. Individual dogs in the same related family have similar appearances and temperaments. As you interview each breeder, discuss his Wolfhounds to learn what you can expect of a dog from his lines. He should be knowledgeable about the breed and about his line. Good breeders welcome questions and will take time to answer them.

Visit with a breeder's dogs to see if you like them.

Ask the breeder about Irish Wolfhound health problems in general and which ones he has encountered. Any breeder who has been breeding awhile has encountered some. Breeders who claim their dogs have never had any problems either have not been breeding very long or are not being candid with you.

Responsible breeders invest a great deal in their dogs and are interested in placing their Wolfhound puppies in the best homes they can find. To this purpose, they will ask you many questions. If a breeder isn't picky, go elsewhere.

The rapport between you and the breeder is as important as the breeder's knowledge, information, and the quality of his dogs and puppies. The breeder will be a resource for you for the life of the dog. He needs to be someone you are comfortable with, can talk to, and can trust.

How a Breeder Will Evaluate You

Reputable breeders are protective of the breed and their dogs. They want homes where each puppy will be well taken care of for life. They will interview you to determine if you are one of the homes they are looking for. Even though good breeders are willing to take back any of their puppies at any time, they would prefer not to. Therefore, breeders look for indicators of potential problems and of likely success.

The responsible Wolfhound breeder will seek information about your family and if everyone in the family wants a Wolfhound. The breeder wants a home where the puppy will be included in all appropriate household activities.

The breeder will be interested in the other dogs you have had and what their lives were like. Although it isn't required that you have had dogs before, if you have, the breeder can get an idea of the life you offer your dog. The breeder will also want to know about other pets you have now, including dogs, cats, birds, and other creatures.

The breeder will want to learn about your home and yard and will probably want your Wolfhound to live as a housedog. Most breeders will only place puppies with families that have sturdy aboveground fences. Although you don't need acreage, the yard needs to be big enough for a giant dog to run and exercise. The house doesn't need to be a palace, but it should be adequate to accommodate an adult Wolfhound.

Wolfhound breeders who live close enough may ask to visit your home. If the breeder lives too far away, he may have a friend in your area who can visit you. This is done because some puppy buyers will misrepresent themselves to breeders in an effort to get a puppy— something you would never do. A home visit assures the breeder that your home is indeed a good one for one of his puppies.

Expect to provide the information; go elsewhere if the breeder is not interested in you and your home. The reputable breeders are the ones with the good puppies, and they are choosy in selecting homes for their puppies.

The breeder will want to know if you want a pet puppy or a show puppy. Although all the puppies will be pets in living with and being a part of a loving family, the designation "pet" means that the puppy isn't intended to be bred or to compete in AKC conformation dog shows. A breeder may evaluate some puppies in the litter as having show potential. He will either keep one or more of these or sell them to people who commit to show the dog to its . AKC championship. Show puppies are given full AKC registration.

If the puppy is sold as a pet, the breeder may provide limited AKC registration. With limited registration, your dog can participate in all AKC events except conformation dog shows. If dogs with limited registration have puppies, those puppies cannot be registered with AKC. Some breeders require that pet puppies be spayed or neutered. They may keep the AKC papers for pet puppies until they receive proof that the Wolfhound has been altered.

All breeders evaluate their puppies at a very young age, often two to three months; but all they can determine at that age is the puppy's potential. Because it is a giant breed, the Wolfhound can change dramatically as he grows. Your pet puppy may develop into show quality. In this case, if you and your breeder agree, the breeder can change the limited

The ears of this six-week-old puppy will not assume the typical "rose" shape until the puppy reaches four months.

registration to full AKC registration. This will allow your dog to compete at AKC dog shows in an effort to earn a championship.

So You Want a Puppy

Most people seeking an Irish Wolfhound want a puppy. Puppies are incredibly cute and appealing. You meet the breeder, the puppy's mother, and probably other relatives of the puppy to get a good idea of how the puppy will look and act as an adult. Starting with a puppy also means you will probably have more years to share with your Wolfhound.

You can raise a puppy from a young age, providing your own training and either avoiding problems or giving gentle corrections for any problems that may occur. You can guide the Wolfhound in the ways of your family.

There are disadvantages to getting a puppy, too. You must train your puppy about housebreaking, puppy chewing, basic house and people manners, and socialization. Although this training is a required chore with a puppy, it can usually be avoided with an adult. Puppies are more active than adults and require more exercise and supervision. Because most people want a puppy, they are often more expensive to purchase than pet adults. Puppies are also more expensive because of the inoculations they need.

How About an Adult Wolfhound?

If you don't have the time or inclination to provide puppy training, consider getting an adult Wolfhound. An adult will most likely be housebroken and trained with house manners or more. With a grown dog, you can see its

═══════ **T I P** ═══════

Giant Puppy Maturation

Puppies develop in well-defined stages, each defined by the senses that begin functioning, the behaviors learned and displayed, and the reactions to different stimuli. Because of this staged development, puppies must stay with their mother and littermates for the first seven weeks. Giant breed maturation periods may last longer than those of smaller breeds. Most Wolfhound breeders wait until puppies are ten to twelve weeks old before placing them in their new homes.

Children and puppies are a natural combination, but they should be supervised so neither gets hurt.

personality, temperament, and behavior before you take the dog. When you get a puppy, you can only estimate its future adult personality. Adults are calmer and less active than puppies and need less exercise.

A gray area between puppy and adult is an older puppy or adolescent. These can offer some of the benefits of each, in having some training, but they are still not fully mature.

One advantage of seeking an adult Wolfhound is that you are more likely to find one more quickly than you can get a puppy. With a puppy, you may have to wait for a litter to be born and grow to ten to twelve weeks. On the other hand, there may be adults available immediately that need your love and care.

Some people believe that if they get an adult, the dog will not bond with them. This is not true. Wolfhounds are not a "one-person" dog. Most will bond with anyone who shows them kindness and love.

Other people believe that you won't be able to train an adult dog. This, also, is not true. Wolfhounds of any age can learn and be trained. The main challenge is for the owner to learn how to train the dog, and this is true regardless of the age of the dog.

The biggest downside in getting an adult is the shorter life span. You probably won't have the adult as long as you would have a puppy.

Where to Get an Adult Wolfhound

Reputable Wolfhound breeders are an excellent source for older puppies and adults as well as puppies. Most breeders have many dogs, and if a wonderful home comes along, they may be willing to let one go. They may have kept a puppy to show that didn't mature as expected. Perhaps the dog doesn't like to show or has some feature that would be negative for a show career. It can still be an excellent pet.

Remember that reputable breeders will take back a dog at any age and for any reason. Sometimes, a Wolfhound is returned due to no fault of her own. The original owner may have died, gone through a divorce, lost a job, or had to move and couldn't take the dog. The dog is returned to the breeder who would like to be able to find another good pet home for the dog.

Rescue

Most dog breeds, including Irish Wolfhounds, have people who provide a safety net for unwanted dogs. These "rescue" people take in Wolfhounds who can no longer be kept by their owners and then look for new homes for them. The common reasons noted for giving a Wolfhound to rescue are either size or expense.

Some of the dogs in rescue are very adoptable if suitable homes can be found. They are healthy, well mannered, and loving.

Other dogs may have a problem that is the fault of the previous owner. The Wolfhound may not have been trained or socialized. She may not have been allowed in the house when she got too big. She may not have been groomed or taken care of. She may have run off because the yard wasn't adequately fenced. Most rescues are a result of problem owners. With a little training and tender loving care, these Wolfhounds can be wonderful pets.

The rescue people should be able to provide you with information about the Wolfhound that you are considering for adoption. They can tell you what kind of home she came from, if she is good with children, and if she is trust-

Most adults can adjust easily to a new home that offers them the love and good care they all deserve.

worthy with cats and small dogs. They should have a good impression of her temperament and personality.

You may offer to foster a Wolfhound who is available for adoption. Foster homes are usually in short supply. When you foster a Wolfhound, the dog lives with you and you care for her on a temporary basis, until a permanent home can be found. Who knows? You might become the Wolfhound's permanent home.

Male or Female?

Many people have strong preferences about their dog's gender, although either a male or female will make a fine pet. The main difference between Wolfhound males and females is size, and with Wolfhounds, the difference is substantial. The males are substantially bigger, perhaps 4–6 inches (10–15 cm) taller as adults and 40–70 pounds (18–32 kg) heavier.

Some people are concerned that the males may want to wander to find girlfriends. Others don't want to deal with the female's twice-yearly season, when she has a discharge and is receptive to being bred. The easiest way to deal with this, if you have a pet that you don't intend to show or breed, is to spay the girls and neuter the boys. Altering your pet can avoid health problems that affect only intact dogs.

There are probably more differences among individual Wolfhounds because of their unique personalities than because of their gender. That said, in general, the boys usually want to stay closer to you and want more attention than the girls. The girls are affectionate, but the boys need a bit more. The boys are more likely to follow you when you move from room to room, to the kitchen, to the bathroom, or into the shower. As with some other animals, females are better hunters than males and are more likely to enjoy a chase.

Access AKC

AKC's web site at *www.akc.org* can help your search for a breeder. From the home page, click the **Breed** link, then select **Breeder Referral**. On that page, find the **Irish Wolfhound** for information about the Irish Wolfhound Club of America.

To find contacts for local kennel clubs, click the **Clubs** link and select **Club Search**. Next select **Conformation Clubs**, then your state, and **Search**. It will return a list of AKC clubs in your state. Contact the clubs near you. Ask if they know of Irish Wolfhound breeders in your area whom they would recommend.

AKC's web site includes online classified ads, a relatively new feature. Ads can be placed only for litters that have been registered by AKC. A link is also available to breeder ads in the *AKC Gazette*, the organization's monthly magazine. The *AKC Gazette* ads list breeders who may or may not have litters currently.

Access the Irish Wolfhound Club of America Web Site

The IWCA site (*www.iwclubofamerica.org*) should be the most helpful resource in providing information about the breed and in finding a breeder. A contact person who can send you educational brochures on the breed is listed.

Scroll to the portion of the home page titled **Contact Information**. Click on **Breed Contacts**. Scroll to your state to find the name and phone number of one or more people who are willing to discuss Wolfhounds with you and help you find a reputable breeder.

You can click on **US Regional Clubs** or **Clubs Abroad** to identify the clubs closest to you. Lists of the web sites of Irish Wolfhound affiliate clubs in the United States or of those of other countries will be displayed. These sites will also provide leads to breeders.

Click on the link for the current year's national specialty. The IWCA holds a national level show each year in different locations around the country. If it is close to you or you are so inclined, attending the national specialty is the best way to see more Wolfhounds and meet more Wolfhound breeders and owners than you could any other way. There are lure coursing, obedience, agility, and conformation competitions. There are puppy compe-

Be careful when searching online for an Irish Wolfhound. There is much misinformation on the Internet amid the helpful information.

THE INTERNET

titions and educational programs. Hundreds of Wolfhounds and breeders and owners from all over the country congregate to celebrate and compare their hounds. You can see and learn more in a few days here than you can anywhere else.

Find Wolfhounds at Dog Shows

Many Wolfhound breeders and owners exhibit their dogs at AKC dog shows. Shows are an excellent place to meet the people and their dogs.

First, you need to find the dog shows. Go back to AKC's web site. Click on **Events** and in the next window click on **Conformation**. Click on **Events and Awards Search**. Specify the time frame and the state, then click **Search Events**. Review the list for shows in locations convenient for you.

When you click on the name of the show, you will learn when and where the show will be held. It will also name a superintendent, an organization that does much of the work of putting on the show. More information about the show can be found at the superintendent's web site.

Select **Events**, then **Conformation**, and then **Superintendents** to display a page with a link to a list of superintendents. Most superintendents have a web site where you can find more information about the shows that you'd like to attend.

About a week before the show at the superintendent's web site, you can see a judging schedule which will tell you how many

Dog shows that have drawn sizable entries of Irish Wolfhounds are excellent places to meet Wolfhounds, their owners, and breeders.

Wolfhounds are entered, the time at which they will be shown, and the ring in which they will be shown. Note that not every show will have Wolfhounds entered, so check before you go. Either the judging schedule or premium list should have directions to the show.

Some shows charge a nominal admission, but many do not. Most charge for parking. But overall, a dog show is a relatively inexpensive excursion and a wonderful introduction to the world of dogs.

No Web Access?

If you don't have a computer or access to one, you can phone the AKC or the IWCA. Additional contact information is given on page 92 of this book.

BRINGING YOUR WOLFHOUND HOME

Bringing your Wolfhound home shouldn't be a production. It should be as unstressful as you can make it. Your new dog doesn't know why he's traveling away from his family and all that he knows to a new home with strangers.

Preparing Your Home

Examine your home from your Wolfhound's perspective, and puppy-proof your home and yard.

Decide if your new puppy will have access to your whole house or initially be restricted to a few rooms only. Baby gates are effective barriers to keep your Wolfhound in or out of a room, even when the dog is tall enough to look over them. Wolfhounds need to learn to respect fences early.

Look at the room at dog level. Remove breakables, knick-knacks, or valuables that a puppy might damage. Puppies, like other babies, explore the world with their mouths.

Before bringing your Irish Wolfhound puppy home, check your house and yard and remove anything that might be hazardous.

Your Wolfhound's wagging tail can clear a table. A playful puppy can bump into things. Avoid problems by removing what you don't want your puppy to chew or knock over.

Consider doors that may be problems. A running puppy can push through a screen door and escape. Until puppies are familiar with clear glass doors, they can run into one at full speed and get hurt.

Household cleaners and poisonous plants are dangers to your curious Wolfhound. Store cleaning products, antifreeze, insecticides, and drugs in cabinets behind doors the puppy can't open. Chocolate is poisonous to dogs, so keep chocolate well out of reach, too. Make sure the dog cannot get into the garbage.

Keep poisonous plants either out of the house or up very high. Outside, toxic plants must be outside of the yard in which the

Check His Collar

At least once each week, check that the collar is still big enough for your rapidly growing Wolfhound. He will grow through many different sizes. You need to easily fit two fingers under the non-choke-style collar. Slip-style collars should slip easily over his head and rest loosely at the base of his neck. If not, either loosen the adjustable collar or get a larger one.

Your Wolfhound may use all these collars during his life. A quick clip adjustable collar is a good first collar for a puppy, for you can make it larger as he grows.

Wolfhound exercises. While you're in the yard, make sure that your fence is sturdy and that there is no way for the puppy to go over, under, or through it. Especially check for low spots at the bottom of the fence that your puppy could excavate into a full hole and escape.

What to Get Before Your Wolfhound Arrives

Two types of collars are useful for your Wolfhound. A quick clip adjustable collar can be enlarged to some degree to accommodate your growing puppy, so you won't have to buy many as your dog grows. Use it when going on walks provided that you are absolutely sure your pup can't slip out of it. For this reason, slip (choke) collars (metal or nylon) are good to use for walks.

Slip collars must **never** be left on the dog after the walk or training session. Some *Wolfhounders* prefer their dogs to wear no collar at home. There are documented cases where dogs have strangled from mishaps with collars, either getting one hooked on something or when playing with another dog.

Many people getting a giant dog purchase an industrial strength collar and lead. However, a single thickness, 5/8-inch (16-mm) wide nylon collar and 6-foot (2-m) long, 5/8-inch (16-mm) wide nylon lead are perfectly serviceable and quite comfortable for both you and your Wolfhound.

You will need two dishes—one for food and one for water. Five-quart (4.7 L) stainless steel bowls are an appropriate size, easy to clean, and won't chip or break. Initially, feed the puppy the same food prepared in the same manner as that at the breeder's.

Crates

Some Wolfhound owners use crates; others don't. A crate makes puppy raising almost easy. A crate provides a private place where the puppy—and adult—can go to relax and get away for awhile. It greatly speeds housebreaking

Exercise pens, baby gates, and crates are useful to limit your Irish Wolfhound's access to parts of your home while he is getting adjusted.

because dogs do not want to soil their beds. It works as a crib or playpen does for a human baby. Your dog can be safe and out of trouble in the crate when you cannot be there. Make sure you get a crate that is sized for an adult Wolfhound: at least 3 feet (91 cm) tall, 4 feet (122 cm) deep, and 30 inches (75 cm) wide.

Some Wolfhound owners use an exercise pen (ex-pen) to confine their Wolfhound puppies. An ex-pen is a portable fence of hinged panels that can be used to corral the puppy in or away from things the puppy shouldn't have access to.

The bed you select for your dog should be soft and thick to cushion the dog's elbows and other areas where the bones are close to the surface. Get one big enough for an adult Wolfhound. If used in a crate, the bed should fit in the bottom of the crate.

Toys

Puppies chew. But some products intended for dogs can be dangerous for your Wolfhound. Rawhide products, pigs' ears, and hoofs can be swallowed and are not digestible. Giving your dog these products may lead to surgery to extract them from the dog's stomach or intestines.

Provide large knucklebones instead, but take them away when they become small enough for your puppy to swallow. Another good choice is sterilized natural bones that are hollow and sometimes flavored. They can be offered "as is" or can be filled with peanut but-

ter or cheese spread, giving the puppy the long happy chore of extracting the goodies.

It is tempting to load up on toys for the new family member. Fleece and rope toys are fun, as are balls that are too large to be swallowed. Wolfhounds can swallow some very large objects, including giant rope toys and large stuffed animals, so monitor your dog's play. Some Wolfhounds enjoy stuffed animals; others gut them, with the fluffy stuffing spread everywhere. If you get stuffed toys, make sure there are no small parts, such as eyes or buttons, that can be chewed off and swallowed.

Remember that Wolfhounds, like children, quickly tire of new toys. With a little imagination, you can provide a new toy every day or two. A fruit or vegetable such as an orange, apple, carrot, or potato (cut out the eyes) is a flavored toy to toss and chase. Empty boxes are

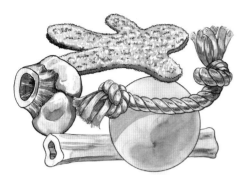

Make certain your Wolfhound's toys are too big to swallow.

great to explore, smash, and shred. Empty plastic bottles bounce in odd directions. When the puppy is done with the "toy," you can throw it away. Don't use shoes or socks as toys, however, or anything else you normally wouldn't want the puppy to play with. Most puppies don't know the difference between toy shoes and good ones.

Looking Good!

Some basic grooming products are good to have on hand. See the chapter on "Caring for and Feeding Your Irish Wolfhound" for the grooming implements you will need.

Your Wolfhound Puppy Arrives

Your Wolfhound will likely arrive by car or by plane. Arrange for the puppy to travel with a towel or something similar that is strong in the smells of his mother and littermates. If by car, the safest way for your puppy to ride is in a crate. If you haven't a crate, make sure there are two people in the car, one to drive and the other to tend to the puppy. If it is a long ride, schedule potty breaks along the way.

Wolfhounds that arrive by plane will travel in an airline-approved crate. It must be big enough for the puppy to stand up and turn around. If at all possible, get a nonstop flight. Consider the time of day of the flight. Midday is warmer for winter flights, and very early morning flights are cooler for summer. Flights later in the day are more likely to be delayed or canceled, so they are less desirable for puppy flights. The airline will tell you what you need in terms of health certificates, arrival times and locations, and any limitations it has. Make your arrangements early.

Now He's Here

Plan for your Wolfhound puppy to arrive when someone can be home full time for his first several days in your home. Don't schedule the homecoming around holidays or when the basic routine of your household will be more hectic than normal. The transition to your home should be as uneventful for the puppy as possible.

When your new puppy arrives home, take him first to the place you want him to use for his bathroom. Let him wander around and sniff. It may take awhile, but if he hasn't gone recently, he will eventually relieve himself. Praise him calmly while he is in the process or just after he finishes.

Offer him a drink of water. With supervision, let him investigate the yard and rooms he will have access to. Introduce him to the other members of the family, making sure that no one overwhelms the puppy. Introduce him to other pets gradually; monitor the meetings to avoid mishap.

Wolfhound puppies sleep a lot, and it will soon be time for a nap. Put your puppy in his crate or bed with the towel that smells like his previous family. Give him undisturbed time to sleep, without people or other pets bothering him. If you use a crate and he fusses, assume initially that he needs to go, and take him out. If he still fusses after he has relieved himself, ignore him. If you keep responding to his fussing when he has gone to the bathroom recently, he is training you to come play with him when he calls.

Housebreaking

Put your Wolfhound puppy's crate/bed near the door he will use to go out to potty. When he begins to awake from his nap, whoosh him outside to relieve himself. Don't paper train a Wolfhound puppy. First, it takes too much paper; second, you must break the paper habit when you train him to go outside. Dogs are creatures of habit. If you make sure that he always goes in a certain place in your yard, he will seek that place to go to when he feels the need. Avoiding accidents not only avoids a mess to clean up, but it avoids imprinting on the puppy's mind a place to relieve himself that is unacceptable to you.

The secret of successful housebreaking is getting your puppy outside when he has to go: immediately when he wakes up, after eating, and during play when he pauses to go, sometimes sniffing first. Watch closely during play, for you may have a few seconds to get him outside. If you use a crate, he will let you know

Put your puppy's crate inside your house, not outdoors. This crate will shortly be too small for a growing Irish Wolfhound puppy.

when he wants to go because he doesn't want to soil his bed. You will have only a few seconds because a puppy doesn't have much time between recognizing the need and going.

Another housebreaking aid is to put your new puppy's food and water on a rigid schedule. What goes in on time comes out on time.

Establish exact times when your Wolfhound puppy gets meals and water (four times a day, for example). These times apply on weekends, too; you cannot sleep in until your puppy is reliably housebroken. No snacking or drinking in between. Soon, you will know your puppy's personal schedule and can make sure he gets

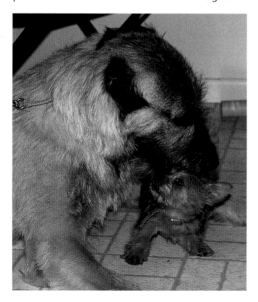

to the chosen place to potty when needed. Extra vigilance when he is quite young will reward you with a puppy that is housebroken very quickly.

Early Training

The best way to prevent problems with your Wolfhound is to avoid his starting bad habits. If he doesn't have the opportunity to get into trouble, he is less likely to do so later. This takes more monitoring by you when he is a baby. This is where the crate and ex-pen are such boons. When you cannot watch him, confine him to his bed in the crate or ex-pen. Take him out to potty, play with him, groom him, and pet him, then put him back in the crate for a nap.

As he grows, little by little, gradually give him more freedom as he earns it, as you would a child. First, let him alone for a few minutes without watching him. Progress to going into the next room for a short time without confining him. If you go too fast and he slips, take a step back and restore some of the old limit.

Puppies, like babies, explore with their mouths; they played with their littermates with their mouths. It is only natural that they may play with you and your family that way. This must be stopped when it starts. If the puppy puts his mouth on your body, clasp his muzzle, give it a shake, and say "No!" sternly. He must learn early that he shouldn't put a mouth on a person. This normally isn't a problem with a Wolfhound, but if you notice it, correct it right away.

Introduce your Irish Wolfhound to other dogs, especially smaller dogs, with careful supervision.

Don't assume that Irish Wolfhounds and horses will get along because they are both large animals; having them meet through a fence provides some safety for both.

Don't allow him to do as a puppy anything you do not want him to do as an adult. Some people allow their Wolfhound on their furniture and in their bed. But if that is not your plan, don't invite him on the furniture as a puppy.

It is useful to teach a puppy that it is acceptable for someone to interfere with his eating. You needn't do this with a slow, reluctant eater. But if the dog is a fast eater or might protect his food, it is an important lesson. While the puppy is eating, add a special treat, a bit of cheese or meat, to his bowl with your hand. Do this a couple of times during the meal. After he has accepted your doing it, if you have a child, let the child do it. He will learn that he need not protect his food, for if a person puts her hand in his bowl, an extra treat appears.

Exuberant puppies will jump up on you to play and get your attention. When your puppy jumps on you, grab his front paws—and hold them. He will squirm, pull away, perhaps bite at your hands. Hold on. After a full 30 or 60 seconds, let go. After two or three times, the puppy will still jump, but not close enough for you to grab his feet. The result is, he no longer jumps on you. Note that the situation corrects his behavior; he cleverly figures out how to prevent you from grabbing his feet.

When correcting a puppy, the correction must be sufficient and immediate. The puppy will not connect a correction with the bad action if the correction happens later. You must catch your puppy in the act. When you discover that he has chewed the couch and

start scolding him, he is responding to your current displeasure; he is not acting guilty for destroying the couch.

One last caveat: **Don't ever** correct a dog for coming to you when you call, no matter what the dog has done. If you do, you are teaching him not to come to you. Conversely, don't ever call your dog to you to do anything the dog thinks is unpleasant, such as getting a bath, a pill, or his toenails clipped. If you are going to do one of these activities, you go and get your dog.

Introducing Your Wolfhound to Your World

One of the first trips for your Wolfhound will be to your veterinarian for a checkup and inoculations. While there, get your puppy microchipped and registered in a national canine identification registry. Hopefully, your puppy will never escape from your yard or during a walk. If this happens, Wolfhounds can get very far away very fast. Some Wolfhounds are wary of strangers and may be difficult to catch. But when someone does catch up with them, the microchip will enable authorities to identify and return these lost pets.

Short neighborhood walks will introduce your new puppy to new people, places, and perhaps other animals. Remember that your puppy will always need to be on lead, even if you live in a safe area. Keep the walks short, for puppies tire easily.

To accustom your Wolfhound to walking on a lead, just let him walk around with the lead on. You go where he walks. Progress to standing by his right side facing in the same direction. When he walks, you walk with him. When he stops, position yourself again to his right and facing the same direction. Again, walk with him when he goes. You'll soon find that

he will walk with you, because that is what he thinks he has been doing.

Neighborhood walks and visits to parks are great opportunities to socialize your puppy. Wolfhounds attract people. Encourage him to meet new people. Let them pet and talk to him. If he seems unsure, you can carry some extra tasty treats, like cheese or bits of meat. Sneak a treat to the friendly stranger to offer your puppy. He will discover that these nice new people are the source of wonderful goodies.

Don't comfort a shy puppy with a cooing voice, for you are then reinforcing a behavior you don't want. Act confident yourself, ignore his hesitancy, but don't push him. He will take his cue from you, his leader, and become more confident.

Wolfhounds usually like other dogs. If there are friendly dogs available on your walks, you can have them meet your dog. Make sure, though, that both dogs are under the control of their people, so that no one takes offense or misbehaves.

Dog clubs in your area may offer puppy kindergarten classes. At these classes, your Wolfhound gets to meet other people and dogs and gets the beginning of gentle obedience training.

Whenever possible, take your Wolfhound with you wherever you go. Plan your leisure to include your puppy. The more positive experiences he has as a youngster, the more confident, well adjusted, and cosmopolitan he will be as an adult.

Be aware of potential problems and deal with them before they happen: a Wolfhound could go over a railing of this height very easily.

Even an older puppy may grow too large for people not prepared to own and care for an Irish Wolfhound. Sadly, such dogs may be turned over to rescue.

Your Wolfhound Adult Arrives

Many concepts for bringing a puppy home also apply for an adult Wolfhound.

With an adult you can know more about his personality and habits. He is probably house-broken and will more quickly learn the location of the "spot."

At first, your adult Wolfhound will not be accustomed to your household routine. You must introduce him to them slowly, allowing him to investigate at his own pace.

He may not have lived with small children or any children, The increased sound level and higher energy of some children can startle a dog from a quieter home, so watch his reactions.

If he seems stressed, keep youngsters quiet and slow-moving as he learns about them.

Time out in crate or bed can help him better acclimatize.

Introduce other pets to an adult Wolfhound slowly. Most Wolfhounds enjoy the company of dogs, so any non-aggressive dogs in the home should be no problem. Introduce them in a neutral space with both on leads.

If the adult Wolfhound is unaccustomed to cats and you have any, it may pose a problem as he may chase cats that run. You can sepa-rate them at first. If he tends to chase the cats, don't let them outside together and monitor them indoors. Give the cats a place to escape to where the Wolfhound cannot catch them.

When he first joins your home, accept his habits during the transition. Gradually introduce your routine, and he will adjust and enjoy his new home. Your adult will happily bond with you if treated kindly, fairly, and with respect.

CARING FOR AND FEEDING YOUR IRISH WOLFHOUND

The care you give your Irish Wolfhound will have a significant impact on her quality of life and on whether she will reach her full potential.

What to Feed

Irish Wolfhounds should be fed a premium kibble that has consistently high quality ingredients. Remember that stipulating "protein" content is not sufficient. Animal hair, nails, and feathers are protein. Your breeder or veterinarian can recommend some premium brands.

Most quality brands offer several formulas to suit your dog's situation and lifestyle, such as "maintenance," "performance," and "senior." Several premium brands have foods specifically formulated for large breeds; these are suitable for Irish Wolfhound adults. Some companies make a large breed puppy food that has high quality ingredients and is balanced for a fast growing giant puppy.

Whether groomed for a show or not, a well-cared-for Irish Wolfhound will always be happy and healthy.

Don't ever feed an Irish Wolfhound puppy regular puppy food. The calorie and protein levels are too high. Your Wolfhound puppy should not be given high levels of protein or supplements, especially calcium, to boost her growth. Such supplements cause more problems than they solve. Recent studies indicate that high fat (above 16 percent), high calorie, and high calcium (above 1 percent) found in regular puppy food are likely to produce skeletal abnormalities in large breed puppies. If premium large breed puppy food is not available in your area, it is far better to feed premium brand adult food than puppy food.

Your Irish Wolfhound puppy will grow very fast naturally. HOD (hypertrophic osteodystrophy), panosteitis, OCD (osteochondritis dissecans), and hip dysplasia are among the bone and joint disorders that can be caused by high protein levels, supplements, and super-enriched

TIP

Vitamin C

Some breeders recommend vitamin C for growing puppies. Although it may not do any good, it should do no harm. Vitamin C is water soluble, and whatever the dog doesn't use will be expelled in her urine. Make sure that the vitamin C is not buffered, however, for the buffering contains calcium, and you may be inadvertently supplementing the puppy with calcium when giving the vitamin C.

foods. It is much better for your fast growing giant to grow slowly. In addition, it is less stressful on her body to be somewhat slender rather than plump. She will get as big as she is genetically entitled to be, which is pretty big, and she will be healthier when not pushed to grow bigger faster.

Kibble can be fed with or without water added, whichever your dog prefers. If you feed it dry, the food won't spoil if your dog doesn't finish her meal right away. You may add some canned dog food for added flavor if your dog isn't a hearty eater. Do not add table scraps. They unbalance the well-balanced dog food and tend to produce overweight dogs.

Fresh water is important to your dog's health. When housebreaking your puppy, however, you may want to provide water at specific regulated times. Remember that what goes in on schedule comes out on schedule. Giving food and water at the same times each day helps to regulate the puppy's digestion and speeds housebreaking.

Your senior Irish Wolfhound has special dietary needs, too. Because her metabolism and activity level slow down, the challenge is to provide high quality food with sufficient protein to keep the body in good repair, while not letting the dog get overweight. Many premium brands make special foods for the older dog. If your Wolfhound has a specific health problem, your veterinarian can prescribe a diet that may help.

If you change dog foods, do so gradually over several days to a week, serving a mix of

Your Wolfhound's access to clean fresh water needn't be this elaborate, but he'll need to drink several times a day. Remember to clean the water bowl regularly.

the old and new food. This gradual change helps avoid digestive upsets, including diarrhea.

How to Feed

Five-quart (4.7-L) stainless steel dog bowls are excellent for both food and water. Plastic bowls can be chewed or can crack and are more difficult to clean. Glass and ceramic bowls can chip or break, with risk of injury.

Until recently, it was recommended that giant breeds like Irish Wolfhounds be fed with their food bowls raised 1–2 feet (30–60 cm) above the floor. Recent studies, however, indicate that there is a positive correlation between bloat (see the chapter "Your Irish Wolfhound's Health") and dogs being fed from raised dishes. So we are putting the food bowls back on the floor.

The exception to this is older dogs or those with arthritis. It is kinder and more comfortable for these dogs to be fed elevated. You can purchase stands for this purpose. What works equally well are small waste baskets with round openings sized just smaller than the widest part of a 5-quart (4.7-L) stainless steel food bowl.

Adult Irish Wolfhounds should be fed twice a day. In the wild, dogs hunted and faced either feast or famine, depending on their success. With domesticity, twice-a-day feedings put much less stress on your dog's digestive system. Give her the food and allow 10 minutes for her to eat; after that, pick it up.

An alternative to feeding twice a day is free feeding, wherein dry food is available all the time, and the dog nibbles whenever she wants. However, free feeding makes it harder to track how much your dog is eating. It doesn't work

Less active Wolfhounds will normally eat correspondingly less than more energetic ones to maintain a healthy weight.

well for dog gluttons, who only stop eating when the food is gone. It is also inappropriate for multidog homes. Puppies should not free-feed because they can incur bone problems from a high calorie intake, and it makes housebreaking more difficult.

Don't feed your Wolfhound immediately after strenuous activity, and let her rest before and after meals. Although not proven, many believe that vigorous exercise soon before or after eating a meal or drinking a lot of water can increase the chance of bloat.

How Much to Feed

Most Irish Wolfhound adults eat between 6 and 14 cups of kibble per day split between two meals. The amount of food depends on the individual dog's metabolism and activity level.

If you have more than one Wolfhound, you can feed them separately by putting each in either different crates or different rooms to eat their meal.

TIP

Multidog Household

In a multidog household, separate the dogs for feeding. This avoids any potential fights over food. It also enables you to monitor how much food each dog is eating and to know when one is not eating well, which may be a sign of illness.

How much is right for your dog is best learned from your dog: look at her and feel her beneath the coat. The ribs should be covered with flesh, but you should still be able to feel them. She should have a distinct waist. If she is too heavy or too thin, adjust the amount of food you give her.

If you give your Wolfhound treats, remember to include these when determining how much you are feeding each day. If she is heavy, you can continue with the goodies, but reduce the amount of kibble until the extra weight is lost. As with people, doggy obesity can cause health problems and can shorten a dog's life.

Your breeder should tell you how much to feed your puppy when you first get her. If the breeder doesn't provide this information, you can begin feeding a young puppy two to three cups of kibble at each of three daily meals if she is younger than four months old. After the first several days of adjusting to her new home when she may not eat with gusto, if your puppy leaves a lot of food, you can reduce the amount.

If she cleans her plate, however, give her a half-cup more at the next meal. Irish Wolfhound puppies grow very fast and not always evenly. At eight weeks, they are gaining about 3–5 pounds (1.5–2 kg) and about 1/2-inch (1 cm) of height per week. By always providing a bit more food than your growing puppy will eat, you know that she is getting enough. Again, watch that she is not getting chubby.

At about four months, you can divide what she is eating each day into two meals. Some dogs will eat more heartily in the morning or the evening, so adjust the amount you feed at the two meals accordingly. There is no ironclad rule that both meals be exactly the same amount. However, Wolfhounds should never be fed only one meal a day.

The amount of food your Irish Wolfhound will eat increases through adolescence, until about 18 months to 2 years of age. Adolescent males will eat the most. The amount of food eaten will stabilize at a lower amount when they are between two and three years old. Females, who are smaller and mature some-what sooner, may begin eating an adult por-tion sooner than the males.

Senior and less active Wolfhounds need less food. If you notice your couch potato or older dog gaining weight, reduce the amount of food she gets until she is a good healthy weight again. Remember that your senior Wolfhound still needs the same amount of

Walking, whether in a woodland or anywhere else, is great exercise for both you and your Wolfhound.

TIP

Important Reminder

A dog should have only half-sized meals for 24–36 hours after general anesthesia. Dogs of breeds that have the propensity to bloat may do so if fed a full meal after even minor surgery.

good quality protein to maintain good health. Cut calories as necessary, but do so without reducing the quality and amount of protein.

Exercise

Irish Wolfhounds were bred to run. But the Irish Wolfhound is also a laid back breed and doesn't need or want to run all day. Good gal-lops around a sizable fenced yard or a nice walk a couple of times a day is sufficient for

Wolfhounds and other sighthounds love to run and chase.

TIP

Jogging with Your Wolfhound

If you enjoy jogging and want your Wolfhound to join you, wait until she is at least 18 months old. Then, build her up gradually as with any athlete, starting with short distances and progressing to longer ones. And remember to always keep her on lead.

---

an adult Wolfhound. Exercise needs will vary with individual dogs. Wolfhounds from lure coursing lines will run more.

Puppies, on the other hand, can be substantially more active and need more exercise. However, this must always be free exercise where the puppy can stop immediately when

she chooses. This precludes long walks unless you are prepared to carry (or drive) her home if she tires.

Tailor the puppy's exercise to be nontraumatic to her fast growing bones and joints. She should not be allowed to jump, especially to jump down where she will land on her front legs. When she wants to get down from a high place such as a car or van and cannot step down, hold her around her chest as she jumps to cushion the impact, providing a soft landing for her front feet.

Some Wolfhound fanciers also believe that a puppy's running should be in relatively straight paths because zigzagging is traumatic to young elbows and shoulders. Restrict a puppy's romping with bigger, older dogs because the larger dogs can inadvertently hurt the puppy with rough play.

Your Irish Wolfhound must run and play only in a fenced enclosure. Make sure the fence is secure and adequate to prevent the dog from escaping. Invisible (electronic) fences don't work for Wolfhounds. When chasing something, the electric collar isn't a sufficient deterrent. It works only when the dog is wearing the collar. Plus, the invisible fence won't keep intruders out of your dog's yard.

The Irish Wolfhound is a sighthound whose original function was to chase down prey. Although few dogs are used for hunting today, this instinct to chase is a part of her character. This breed cannot be taken on off-lead walks. With no constraints, your Wolfhound may get interested in something, run, and be gone, and will never hear you calling her. Her yard must have an escape-proof fence. It need not be acreage, but it must be secure.

Grooming

An Irish Wolfhound is a rough-coated, Greyhound-like breed. This coat is her crowning glory and one of the defining features of the breed. Coat care is a significant part of grooming your Wolfhound, which also includes care of her ears, nails, and teeth.

The coat is not oily, which means a cleaner dog and home and minimal, if any, doggy odor. If the coat is cared for and the undercoat brushed out when needed, there should be little shedding.

Coat Care

The Irish Wolfhound has a double coat. The outer coat is rough, harsh, wiry, hard to the touch, and longer than the undercoat. The outer coat is longer over the eyes and at the end of the muzzle and under the jaw. The hair on the neck, body, and legs lies fairly flat and

is 3–4 inches (8–10 cm) long. The coat feels crisp and shouldn't be long and silky. The undercoat is shorter, soft, and denser. It is the undercoat that sheds.

A correct Irish Wolfhound coat is not only beautiful and weather resistant, but it is easy to care for. A soft wooly or long silky coat has a greater tendency to mat and tangle. So when

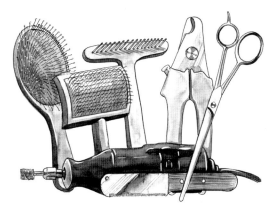

Among the tools you will need to groom your Wolfhound are a pin brush, slicker brush, grooming rake, scissors, and either a nail grinding tool or nail clippers. You may also need a stripping knife.

Regular coat care keeps the dog both clean and beautiful.

you are getting a puppy, try to get one with a good coat, and you will have less work to do.

A 30-minute brushing once or twice a week with a pin brush should keep your Wolfhound's coat in good condition. A pin brush has steel bristles with rounded ends. Many owners also comb through the coat using a steel dog comb to ensure there are no mats. If your dog's coat mats easily, you will have to brush and comb more often. Brushing not only removes dead hair and prevents tangles but also dislodges dirt and debris picked up in the coat and helps keep the dog clean. The beard and moustache need to be brushed and combed daily to keep them clean and tidy. If you don't wipe her face after she eats or drinks, your clever Wolfhound will use your furniture or carpet as a napkin.

When your dog is shedding, she will need to be brushed more often to remove the under-coat. A slicker brush can be used to help remove the dead hair faster. A slicker brush also has steel pins, but they are shorter, curved, and spaced closer together.

Trimming

Normally, the Irish Wolfhound's coat needs little trimming. It should look natural. But a couple of places do need attention.

An Irish Wolfhound can be given a bath oudoors if the weather is warm enough.

Trim the extra hair on her feet between the pads and toes, especially if she walks on slippery surfaces. Untrimmed, the hair underfoot can cause the dog to slip and possibly get hurt.

The hair around a Wolfhound's private parts needs to be trimmed, also, to help keep her clean. This doesn't need to be done frequently, but should be done to keep excrement from getting in the dog's coat. If you don't want to trim the hair yourself, your veterinarian or groomer can do it.

Bathing

You have choices here. If you want to preserve the desired rough, hard coat, don't bathe your Irish Wolfhound often with shampoo and water. Many dogs are never bathed. Brushing and raking keep them clean.

Owners who want a more pristine dog bathe their Wolfhounds more often, once or twice a month. Make sure you use a dog shampoo. Dog hair has a different pH value than human hair. Don't use a crème rinse or softening agent on the coat. The texture and feel of the Wolfhound coat should be harsh and wiry. There are special shampoos for harsh coated dogs that you may use to preserve the coat's texture.

There are waterless shampoos, no-rinse shampoos, and bath wipes available for dogs. These can be used when a full bath is not an option or when you want to limit the number

Clean the inside of your Wolfhound's ears weekly to avoid ear infection and wax buildup.

of baths to retain a good coat. They can also be used to clean the beard and mustache.

Ear Care

Ears should be cleaned about once a month, or more often if your Wolfhound's ears get dirty or have wax buildup. Use ear-cleaning solution or alcohol, cotton balls, and cotton swabs. Dampen a cotton ball with the solution or alcohol. Use the damp cotton ball to clean the inside of the ear leather and in the crevices as far as you can comfortably reach. Use

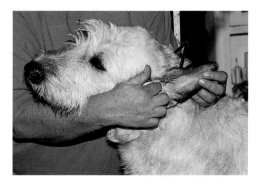

Here is an example of correct head grooming. The hair on the eyebrows, beard, and moustache is longest, with shorter hair on the skull and ears.

cotton swabs to clean the grooves and crevices of the ear that the cotton ball didn't reach.

Teeth

Include weekly toothbrushing in the care of your Irish Wolfhound. A soft toothbrush specially made for dogs and a doggy toothpaste can be used. In a pinch, a soft cloth such as a washcloth can be wrapped around your finger to wipe your dog's teeth. Pay particular attention to the large teeth (molars) at the sides of the mouth. Tartar builds up faster on these teeth. Your veterinarian will examine your dog's teeth during her annual physical and may recommend additional, more thorough, teeth cleaning.

Some bones are marketed to help clean teeth with the chewing. Puppies need bones available when they are teething. Choose bones carefully. Do not give any bone that can splinter or be swallowed. Don't give anything (e.g., hooves or pigs' ears) that is small enough to be swallowed, and take away anything that has been chewed into small pieces. If your Wolfhound can hold the whole item in her mouth, she can swallow it. Don't provide rawhide bones or chews, no matter how much the dog likes them. A Wolfhound can chew off pieces of rawhide and ingest them. These products are not digestible and can block your dog's digestive system, potentially requiring expensive surgery.

Nails

Although no dog likes having her toenails trimmed, trimming her nails is critically important for the health of the feet of your running hound. She uses her nails to grip the ground when running, but the nails should not be close to touching the ground when she is standing. If they are, the dog rocks back on her feet, the toes flatten, spread, and splay. Those feet support a big dog; they must be kept functional.

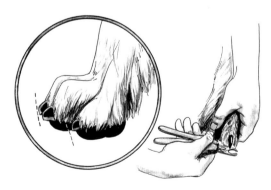

Trim your dog's nails as close to the quick as possible without cutting into the live area.

Keep the Coagulant Close

If you cut the quick and the dog's nail bleeds, styptic powder put on the nail will stop the bleeding. In an emergency, unflavored gelatin also works as well.

It is best to trim a dog's nails every few weeks. With the hair on the foot, it is easy not to notice the nail length until they get too long. The quick (the blood vessel) that grows into the nail will grow further into the nail if you let the nails get too long. If this happens, when you cut them, the nails will bleed. You can keep the quick back by trimming the nails regularly.

You can use two types of tools to cut your dog's nails. One option is a dog nail clipper. It must be one designed for giant dogs. Wolfhounds have big nails that won't fit in smaller clippers. The other alternative is an electric grinder type pet nail groomer with a sandpaper drum (about 1/2-inch [1 cm] in diameter) that spins and files the nail shorter.

The electric nail grinder is more expensive. But dogs mind it less because it doesn't pinch the nail as the clipper does. With the grinder, it is also easier to avoid cutting the quick. If you cannot trim your dog's nails, take her to a groomer to get the job done.

And So to Bed

Irish Wolfhounds are prone to calluses and hygromas (see the chapter on "Your Irish Wolfhound's Health") on their elbows and other areas where the bone is close to the skin and bears weight when they lie down. To avoid these and other problems, your Wolfhound should have a soft cushiony surface to lie on.

If you allow it, most Wolfhounds will enjoy sharing your bed and your couch. If you have room, they will settle for a human mattress on the floor. If you buy a dog bed, make sure that it is big enough for an adult Wolfhound to stretch out on and thick enough to provide adequate cushion. One alternative is to get a 4-inch (10-cm) thick piece of foam rubber and wrap it in a sheet. The sheet can easily be removed for laundering.

Make sure your Wolfhound's bed is soft and big enough.

Whether or not you want to show your dog, you may want her to look like a show dog, with a "commanding appearance." Additional attention to the coat can make the dog look as much like the AKC Irish Wolfhound standard as possible.

Stripping

Much of the extra coat work involves a process called "stripping," by which some hair is pulled out to modify the appearance of the dog. It can be done by hand, by grabbing a few of the longer hairs and pulling them out. This can get quite tiring with a dog as big as an Irish Wolfhound, however. It can also be done with a stripping knife in one of two ways. The knife can be run over the top of the coat, removing some of the outer coat. Or, some hair can be grasped between the side of the knife and the thumb and be pulled out. It takes practice and skill to strip the coat to get the desired effect and not leave big holes in the coat.

A rake comb is another tool that can be used for stripping. It also helps by removing dead undercoat. With one to three rows of teeth, it is worked through the coat layer by layer to remove shedding undercoat and tangles. Run across the topcoat, it removes or strips off some of it.

Some Wolfhound owners use a *More* comb for stripping some of the topcoat and for removing the undercoat. The beginner should be careful when using the *More* comb, for too much hair may be removed, leaving holes in the dog's coat.

Small Greyhound-like Ears

The ears are supposed to be small and Greyhound-like. A Greyhound, and therefore the Irish Wolfhound, has a rose ear. A rose ear is a drop ear (folded at the base rather than held erect) that has a second fold in it so that the burr (the irregular formation in the cup of the inside of the ear) is visible. Long or bushy hairs are stripped from the inside, base, and the outside of the ear to enhance its small appearance. This leaves the coat on the outside of the ear leather short, smooth, and flat.

Long, Lean Head

The head should be long and lean and the skull not too broad. To emphasize these characteristics, long hair on the top of the skull is stripped starting from behind the eyebrows. The hair is gradually left a little longer toward the

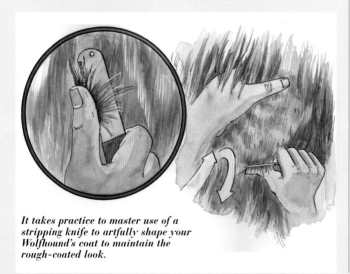

It takes practice to master use of a stripping knife to artfully shape your Wolfhound's coat to maintain the rough-coated look.

IRISH WOLFHOUND COAT

back of the skull and longer still on the neck, blending in gradually on the neck, so that there is no abrupt line between shorter and longer hair. Hair can also be stripped off the cheeks, below the jaw, and the upper part of the neck, again gradually blending into the neck. It may be necessary to remove some bushy hair from the neck, blending into the base of the neck and shoulders. The goal is to accentuate the desired look of a long head and long arched neck. If too bushy, the head and neck will look short and heavy.

An ungroomed Irish Wolfhound can look shaggy.

Taming Bushy Thighs

A Wolfhound's thighs should be long and muscular with stifles (knees) well bent. A well-coated dog can have so much hair on her rear legs that she looks like she is wearing pan-taloons. Excessive undercoat can be stripped away, being careful not to take off too much. Use a picture of a groomed show-quality Irish Wolfhound as your guide to how much hair to remove.

Remember to trim the hair around the feet and between the pads and toes. This is done primarily for safety.

Getting the Correct Underline

An Irish Wolfhound is a Greyhound-type dog and, as such, should have a deep chest and good tuck-up (upward curve) at the abdomen. Brushing the chest hair down and stripping or trimming the belly hair can enhance these characteristics. Again, make sure you blend the coat from one part to another so there is no sharp border between shorter and longer coat.

Your grooming should produce the desired outline of a giant Greyhound-type dog while retaining his rough-coated look. Your Wolfhound should never look overtrimmed or sculpted.

Now that she's so beautifully groomed, get the camera, and take some pictures.

A well-groomed Irish Wolfhound is undeniably impressive.

YOUR IRISH WOLFHOUND'S HEALTH

The health of an Irish Wolfhound can be improved if his owner is knowledgeable and observant, seeks medical help when needed, and has access to competent veterinary care.

Average Life Span

Irish Wolfhounds have a shorter average life span, 6.5 years, than smaller dogs. It is incumbent on a Wolfhound owner to be familiar with the health problems that occur more frequently in the breed. By learning your options and providing good care for your dog, you increase the chance of a longer and healthy life for him. Those dogs that aren't affected by the conditions discussed here and who are well cared for may live to nine or ten years or more. Dogs that die young from osteosarcoma, heart disease, or gastric bloat and torsion lower the averages.

The Observant Owner

The first line of defense for good health for your dog is to notice any changes in him. Dogs

A change in your dog's posture or how he stands could be a sign of illness.

are creatures of habit. It is up to you to notice any deviations that may indicate that your dog is sick. Furthermore, Irish Wolfhounds tend to be stoic and suffer pain and discomfort without complaining. You must be alert to any changes.

Note changes in your dog's eating habits. Is he eating or drinking more, less, or differently than normal? Notice not only what goes in but also what comes out. Is he urinating more or less? Are there changes in the way or frequency in which he defecates or in the form of his stool? Is there any blood in his urine or stool? Dogs vomit more easily than people do; but if he throws up frequently or heaves and nothing comes up, it could be a sign of a serious problem.

Notice any changes in his activity, movement, and posture. Is he more or less active? Does he walk or move in a way that isn't normal for him? Is he lame, stiff, or uncoordinated? Is he depressed, more clinging, more irritable? Does he stand hunched up, with his abdomen tense? Is he breathing differently? Anything not normal in his behavior must be noted.

When you groom your Wolfhound, notice any new bump, lump, sore, or abrasion. Is his coat different? A dog's health shows in his coat. Run your hands over his bones and muscles to detect if they are the same on both sides. If you have an intact male, check that his testicles haven't changed in size or feel. Look for discharge from any orifice, including the penis or vulva. Note any sensitivity or pain when you touch him. Take his temperature if you suspect he is ill. A temperature between 101 and 102°F (38 and 39°C) is normal for a

dog. If your dog's temperature is more than a degree higher or lower than normal, call your veterinarian. If it varies by more than two degrees, take your dog to the veterinarian immediately.

Write down everything you notice and bring the list when you visit the veterinarian. You know your dog best and what is normal for him. The doctor doesn't, and he won't see the subtle changes. Further, the excitement of being at the veterinarian's office may affect your dog's behavior. Your observations and input are critical for the veterinarian to make an accurate diagnosis.

Also observe your dog closely *after* your veterinarian has seen him and prescribed treatment and medication. If your Wolfhound doesn't respond as your veterinarian said to expect, tell her, and schedule a recheck appointment. Don't just wait and hope he will improve.

Choosing Your Veterinarian

Veterinarians vary in their experience and expertise. The Irish Wolfhound Club of America recommends that you use one who is expert in treating Irish Wolfhounds. Contacts available at the IWCA web site can help you find such a veterinarian in your area.

If you cannot find one who is experienced in Wolfhounds, find one in your area who is used by breeders and experienced owners of other sighthounds and giant breeds. Some vets may be less familiar with issues characteristic of sighthounds and giant dogs. For instance, sighthounds are particularly sensitive to sedation and anesthesia. Therefore, the doses given to sighthounds must be less than those given to other breeds. Your veterinarian should also

Weigh your Wolfhound each time you visit your veterinarian and stop by more often just to weigh him. Know his normal healthy weight.

A Irish Wolfhound's coat can hide numerous problems. Check under his coat regularly to find bumps and bruises.

be familiar with the growth stages and dietary needs of a Wolfhound puppy.

A veterinarian who has a large client base of Wolfhounds, sighthounds, and other giant breeds has seen more occurrences of the problems your dog may encounter. She will be more likely to provide a quick and accurate diagnosis and be more familiar with the latest options available. She will be familiar with how a normal giant puppy grows. A good veterinarian is one of the most important elements for maintaining a healthy dog and successfully treating health problems.

When evaluating a veterinarian, ask how emergencies are handled. It is critical that you have access to competent veterinary care outside normal office hours. Your Wolfhound may not conveniently get sick when the doctor is in. If a veterinarian uses an emergency clinic, check it out, too.

Osteosarcoma

Osteosarcoma, the most common bone cancer in dogs, is the leading cause of death for Irish Wolfhounds, based on a study done by Gretchen Bernardi, noted Irish Wolfhound breeder and judge, with the approval of IWCA. It is a life-threatening disease; most dogs that develop it die within a year. Initial symptoms include limping and a lump on a bone. If your dog limps, see your vet right away. Early detection increases the number of treatment options and improves their effectiveness. A bone X-ray

extended a dog's survival time. New procedures with limb-sparing surgery, where a metal plate or rod replaces the cancerous portion of bone, offer the dog the chance to regain the use of the affected limb.

The treatments can relieve pain and increase survival time, but none can be considered cures. The average increased life expectancy that treatment can provide the dog varies from two months to two years.

Many Wolfhound owners choose not to treat the disease aggressively. They opt instead for keeping their dog pain-free until euthanasia is required. Those who adopt this perspective consider it kinder and less invasive for the dog. With current technology, the investment by the dog and owner in treatment may not be worth the limited benefit. However, technology always progresses, so check with your veterinarian about your options, and then consider what is right for you and your dog.

can strongly indicate the disease, but a tumor biopsy is needed for a definite diagnosis.

Osteosarcoma occurs most often in large and giant breeds. It can affect a dog at any age and appears in equal frequency in males and females. It occurs most often in the front legs; the next most common sites are the hind legs and the ribs.

If treatment is done, it should be aggressive and may include radiation and chemotherapy in addition to possible amputation. Because this cancer metastasizes to the lungs, a chest X-ray must be taken before considering surgery. Several chemotherapy protocols have

Heart Disease

Heart failure is the second most common cause of death for Irish Wolfhounds, according to the Bernardi survey. Your vet can check for heart problems by auscultation (listening to the heart with a stethoscope), and if she hears anything suspicious, she can check it out by an electrocardiogram or echocardiogram (ultrasound). Your dog's heart should be checked yearly and before surgery. Your veterinarian may refer you to a cardiac specialist.

See your vet if you see signs that might suggest heart disease. Affected dogs are lethargic, tire easily, breathe rapidly, and cough. Affected dogs may lose weight. The sooner a heart problem is identified, the more treatment options are available.

There are multiple kinds of heart problems, varying from mild with no symptoms to those that may eventually cause the dog's death. They can include murmurs, abnormal rhythms (such as atrial fibrillation), defects in some portion of the heart, and specific heart diseases, such as dilated cardiomyopathy.

Atrial fibrillation (AF) is the most common cardiac rhythm disturbance in Wolfhounds, affecting about 10 percent of the dogs at some point in their lives, the average onset being from four to five years. Most dogs don't have any symptoms. A dog with AF doesn't necessarily develop cardiac disease. However, because most dogs with cardiac disease have atrial fibrillation, it is thought that AF may be an indication that a Wolfhound may develop heart disease. A Wolfhound with AF should not be overexercised or allowed to get too hot. Your veterinarian may prescribe medication.

Dilated cardiomyopathy is a disease in which the heart is enlarged and the heart muscle weak. It is the most common cause of congestive heart failure in Wolfhounds. Signs include weight loss and exercise intolerance. Treatment is directed at strengthening the heart muscle, controlling arrhythmias, and preventing fluid build-up caused by poor circulation.

Early symptoms do not always progress to serious heart disease. Depending on the findings, some treatments, including medications, dietary supplements, and life-style and diet changes, may improve the prognosis. Studies have shown that cardiomyopathy may be improved by giving the dog amino acids taurine and carnitine and supplements vitamin E and coenzyme Q10.

Bloat and Torsion

Bloat occurs when gas builds up in a dog's stomach causing it to expand or bloat. The bloated stomach may twist or wrench. The torsion closes the stomach off from the esophagus and/or small intestine and cuts off the stomach's blood supply. The dog is in pain and will go into shock, and the stomach tissue will begin to die.

Be familiar with the symptoms so you will recognize bloat immediately. The dog will probably retch, but all that will come up is a yellow or pale frothy, viscous substance. A bloating dog's stomach will feel taut; his abdomen and sides may or may not be distended. He will appear to be uncomfortable and depressed.

If you suspect that your dog is bloating, you must get him to a veterinarian immediately. You cannot wait until morning (it usually happens at night) or delay even an hour. If you

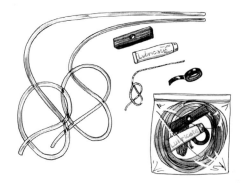

A bloat kit can be used in an emergency to attempt to empty a dog's stomach and relieve the bloat.

═══════ **TIP** ═══════

Giving Liquid Medicine

Put the measured medicine in a syringe which has the needle removed. Pull out the corner of the dog's lip and using the syringe, place the medication as far back as possible between the cheek and the back teeth. With his muzzle tipped up, the dog will swallow the medication.

delay, your dog may die. The veterinarian will treat your dog for shock and take steps to decompress the stomach. If the dog has gone into torsion, surgery is necessary to untwist and empty the stomach. At the end of the surgery, the veterinarian should tack (suture) the dog's stomach to the side of his abdominal cavity to prevent it from twisting again.

Sometimes when the stomach twists, the spleen wrenches; it can also wrench indepen-

dently. In either case, the spleen can be removed because the liver can assume the functions of the spleen. Before removing the spleen, confirm that your veterinarian knows that it should be taken out **without** untwisting it. If the spleen is untwisted, the toxic buildup will be released and the dog will probably die during or shortly after surgery.

The cause of bloat is unknown, although it has been studied for years. It is recommended that a dog not exercise an hour before and after eating. Dogs fed smaller meals more frequently have a lower incidence of bloat. Some suspect that dogs gulp air as they eat. Putting the dog food on the floor, rather than elevated, may slow a fast eater and limit the gulping. Stress probably contributes to bloat. If you think your dog is gassy and may bloat, you can give him a liquid anti-gas product that is primarily simethicone.

A prophylactic gastroplexy or stomach tack may be the best option to avoiding torsion. With gastroplexy, the stomach is sutured to the inside of the body cavity to prevent torsion if the dog bloats. The procedure is scheduled during office hours with a healthy Wolfhound. Although no surgery is risk free, the stomach tack certainly can greatly reduce the danger if the dog bloats. It will almost eliminate the likelihood of torsion, the more serious problem, but it will not prevent bloat. Have the gastroplexy done by a veterinarian with substantial experience doing the procedure and successfully treating dogs with bloat and torsion.

A dog's bloated stomach can be felt at his abdomen, even if distention cannot be seen. Torsion cannot be confirmed without an X-ray.

A well-meaning owner may give an Irish Wolfhound puppy supplements that can cause bone problems as the puppy grows.

Poorly done stomach tacks can tear when the stomach tries to twist, and the stomach may go into torsion in the future after all.

Puppy Bone Problems

Because Wolfhound puppies are growing so fast, they may develop one of the bone diseases that are relatively more common in giant breeds. Supplements or extra-rich foods that encourage fast growth can cause these problems. Keeping a puppy slender can reduce stress on his bones and limit the problems.

Osteochondrosis dissecans is a disease caused by a defect in the process of developing bone from cartilage during rapid bone growth. Pieces of irregularly formed cartilage break off and cause joint pain and swelling. It usually occurs in the joint between the shoulder and upper arm and can also occur in the elbow and other joints; it most commonly occurs between four and eight months of age. The puppy limps and gets worse with exercise. Extending and flexing the joint is painful. An X-ray may show an irregular or loose piece of cartilage. Treatment includes restricting activity and medication for pain. Drugs, including Adequan, are now being used to resolve the problem without surgery. In some cases, however, surgery may be necessary to remove defective and loose cartilage.

Panosteitis ("pano") or wandering lameness is a disease that affects giant puppies between 5 and 12 months old. The cause is unknown, but males are affected more often than females. Pain and lameness shifting from one leg to another over some weeks or months are characteristic of pano. Medication can be given for pain. Exercise should be limited until the puppy grows through the disease, which is self-limiting.

Hypertrophic osteodystrophy (HOD) is characterized by swollen painful joints, usually in the lower leg. It affects giant breed puppies between two and eight months old, and is most normally reported between three and four months. It is often accompanied by a fever. X-rays can confirm the diagnosis. There is some evidence that an infection may contribute to HOD; however, many cases seem to be caused by excess dietary calcium or protein. Treatment includes medications to relieve pain. If the diet is suspect, a change in diet is needed to reduce the calcium or protein. Antibiotics may be given if there is an infection. Even though HOD is very painful, with treatment, the dog can recover.

Hygroma

A hygroma, also called a bursa, may develop when there is repeated trauma to an area of the body where the bone lies close to the surface of the skin. It is a thick serum-filled capsule that

Keep an ongoing record of vaccinations, illnesses, medicines, and medical processes your dog has had.

the body creates to help cushion the area. It usually occurs on elbows but may also appear elsewhere. It can be fairly small, where the hygroma is more felt than seen on the elbow, or it can be as big as a grapefruit or larger.

Hygromas may be avoided by keeping your Wolfhound on a soft, cushioned area. Dogs that lie down hard on a hard surface are more likely to develop hygromas.

Sometimes correcting the dog's environment can allow small hygromas to maintain their size or shrink. Large ones, however, may need to be drained or removed by a veterinarian. One product has proved effective on hygromas and can reduce them without surgery. The operative ingredient to look for is Ichthammol. Applied once or twice a day, it successfully shrinks the hygroma. It may take several days, a week, or longer, depending on the size of the hygroma.

Vaccinations

Many diseases that sickened or killed dogs years ago are now preventable with vaccines: rabies, distemper, canine hepatitis, leptospirosis, and parvovirus. Your Wolfhound puppy will have gotten his initial vaccines while still with his breeder. When you take your puppy for his first visit with your veterinarian, bring the information on the inoculations he has had thus far. Your veterinarian will recommend a series of vaccines and the intervals at which they should be administered. If it is a concern in your area, she will probably include a vaccine against Lyme disease.

There is ongoing discussion within the veterinary and breeder communities on how often dogs need to have booster injections. The traditional view is once a year. Some are finding that every two or three years is sufficient. Drug companies have produced a three-year rabies vaccine that can be used if allowed by your state and local ordinances. Following the vaccination protocol advised by your veterinarian is the best bet for avoiding these diseases.

Dogs that are exposed frequently to other dogs, people, and places should have their immunity boosted once a year. Bordatella vaccine provides protection from kennel cough for only six months, however. Because kennel cough is highly contagious, make sure your dog is current on this vaccine if he will be kenneled or around other dogs.

Heartworm

If there are mosquitoes where you live, your Wolfhound must be on heartworm prevention. When a mosquito carrying heartworm bites your dog, the heartworm larvae are transmitted to the dog. The larvae grow, develop, and migrate in the body for several months and end up as adult heartworms in the dog's heart and lungs. Untreated, they can ultimately kill the dog.

Heartworm can be treated, but it is expensive and hard on the dog. It is far better to give the dog regular heartworm prevention medicine. There are a variety of options for heartworm prevention medication, including monthly tablets and chewables and monthly topicals. These methods are extremely effective, and when they are given on a timely schedule, heartworm infection is completely avoidable. If you have an adult Wolfhound that has not been on heartworm prevention medication, get him checked for heartworms before starting it.

Parasite Control

Fleas and ticks are the most bothersome external parasites. Not only do they annoy you and your Wolfhound and cause skin problems, but they also carry disease. If you have them, you must treat the dog, your home, and your yard simultaneously.

Flea collars aren't successful on Wolfhounds; there is too much dog for the flea collar product to reach. Some topical products available from your veterinarian are effective, including imidacloprid (Advantage) and fipronil (Frontline), which spread to cover the whole dog and kill the fleas when they get on the dog. When treating the house and yard, make sure to use a product that not only kills the adult fleas and ticks, but also the eggs. If you do not, in two weeks, you will have a new infestation.

Rubbing alcohol is toxic to both fleas and ticks. If you find a flea on your dog, you can spray it with rubbing alcohol. If you find a tick attached to your dog, you can spray it with rubbing alcohol first to loosen its grip and then grab it next to the dog's skin, pull it off, and drop it into a bit of alcohol. You can use tweezers if you would rather not handle the ticks. When examining your dog for fleas, flea combs are effective for isolating the fleas and letting you get them. When looking for ticks, make sure you examine inside your dog's ears, where his legs join his body, and on his feet, between his toes and around the pads. You

▬▬ TIP ▬▬

Fighting Fleas

If fleas are a chronic problem, a flea collar in your vacuum cleaner bag will keep them from prospering there.

Be aware of which plants are poisonous to your Wolfhound, and keep them away from your dog.

will need to look and feel through the coat in order to locate ticks.

Internal parasites are primarily intestinal worms: hookworms, tapeworms, roundworms, and whipworms. Often, although not always, when the dog has these worms, your veterinarian can detect them by examining a stool sample under a microscope. You may be able to see bits of white tapeworm (about a quarter to a half inch in length) in your dog's stool. If your dog has diarrhea, have your dog checked for worms or infection. Intestinal worms are usually easily treatable. Heartworm prevention medication should take care of intestinal worms other than tapeworms. Make sure you pick up and dispose of your dog's feces to help avoid spreading worms. Have your dog's stool examined as part of his yearly health checkup.

Spaying and Neutering

If your dog is not going to be shown or bred, it is strongly recommended that the males be neutered and the females spayed. Neutered and spayed dogs can be healthier by avoiding health problems that affect only intact animals. Males will be less inclined to wander, and the females won't cycle through twice-yearly seasons.

There are many opinions on when to get your Wolfhound spayed or neutered. Some veterinarians recommend it be done as puppies, although early spaying can increase the risk of urinary incontinence in females. Others suggest it be done when the dog is about one year old. Some current thought suggests spaying or neutering a dog before sexual maturity may accelerate the dog's growth, which is not good for a Wolfhound because rapid growth exacerbates bone problems.

Your breeder may have preferences, too. Some require that dogs sold as pets be altered. Others may ask you to wait until the dog matures somewhat to determine if he might be successfully shown. Only intact (unaltered) dogs can be entered at AKC dog shows to compete for their championship.

When a dog is spayed or neutered, it is no longer affected by the sex hormones that can affect behavior. Contrary to common opinion, spaying and neutering doesn't make your dog fat; too much food and too little exercise will make your dog fat.

Euthanasia

At the end of their lives, Irish Wolfhounds tend not to linger. They don't have an extended period of geriatric problems that can plague small dogs. At some point, it will be time to say good-bye to your Wolfhound. A gentle passing is the final gift you can give him in return for all the love he has given you.

One hard part is deciding when to have it done. It should be determined by the quality of life the dog has. He doesn't have to bound through fields to have a quality life. If he enjoys lying in the sun, being petted, getting a treat, and is not in much pain, he has a good life. But when discomfort or pain from disease or age is substantial enough to prevent any enjoyment, it is time. His size may also be an issue. A small dog that cannot walk can be carried; a Wolfhound cannot. Your veterinarian may help you decide.

If you can, the kindest way is to stay with the dog when he is euthanized. He will lie on the floor with his head on your lap. With an injection similar to one given prior to surgery, he will

Spayed female and neutered male Irish Wolfhounds are quite happy to be family companions and don't miss anything by not being able to mate.

relax and go to sleep, at last being pain free.

Another big decision is the final resting-place for your dog. You might consider burying your Wolfhound, but that is a large project because of his size. If you bury him on your property, remember that you may move someday. There are pet cemeteries available for you to consider. Many people leave their dog at the veterinarian. But if you do this, you will not know what happens to your Wolfhound. It may vary from a mass grave to a landfill. Consider cremation, which is available through many veterinary practices. You may keep the cremains or bury them.

Long ago, a woman trained sighthounds for a circus act. She told of the dogs living in her home, as part of the family, never having to sleep outside in the rain. She said that when they died, she cremated them. Even then, they never had to sleep outside in the rain.

Some people think large dogs should live outside. Wrong!

All in the Family

Dogs are social animals; banishing them to a solitary life in the yard or garage is cruel. Wolfhounds especially want to be with the family, to be indoors and involved in whatever the family is doing. They are very people oriented and want significant human companionship.

You have already prepared your home for a Wolfhound with earlier suggestions. Having such a tall dog in your home may also involve modifications of your habits.

Counter Surfing

Your Wolfhound can reach any counter or tabletop. You should put food away or not leave it unattended. If you usually defrost meat

Your Wolfhound may learn how to open some of the doors in your home to let herself in or out.

on the counter, you may find it gone before you get to it. If you let the cookies cool on the counter, you may not be the first to try them.

Taking food to the dining room table early will risk your Wolfhound tasting it first. Whole sticks of butter can disappear in a flash, without leaving an oily spot. If you don't clear the table and the counters right after your meal, your Wolfhound may take care of any leftovers.

Don't ever feed your Wolfhound at the table while you are eating or from the counter while you are preparing food. Don't allow anyone else to do so, either. If you do, you will teach her to beg and to expect tidbits. A small begging dog is a nuisance, but a tall dog hovering and looking down on your plate while you are eating is disconcerting.

The tail end of the dog can also clear tables. A happy wagging tail sweeps a moving 3-foot

Be sure your yard is escape-proof both from digging and jumping, so your Irish Wolfhound can safely enjoy being outdoors.

(1-m) radius. Keep breakable and spillable objects well above tail level.

Your Fenced Yard

Your Wolfhound will enjoy romps in the yard, especially if you are there to play with her, but you must make sure it is escape-proof. Not only is a run-away Wolfhound in danger herself, but she may also be a potential nuisance to your neighbors and a potential danger to small pet animals she may chase and injure. If you live in a rural area, your dog can get into serious trouble chasing deer or livestock.

Regularly check the fence to make sure that there is no gap through which she can escape. Some dogs will dig at the base of a fence and soon have a hole big enough to wiggle through. (Strangely, the same sized hole won't be big enough for your dog to return through.)

Before letting your Wolfhound loose in the yard, make certain that all gates are well closed and latched. If service people come into the

yard, they may not close gates securely. Children and even some adults are not always careful about latches. Some Wolfhounds learn how to open gates. You will have to lock these gates. A clip similar to that at the end of a leash can be used to lock most gate latches.

Remember that underground or invisible fences are not appropriate for Wolfhounds. They don't prevent other dogs or people from coming into your yard. A motivated Wolfhound on a chase may well go across the boundary, but the fence will keep the same dog from returning to the yard. Invisible fences won't keep anything out of your yard. A neighbor's small dog or cat may wander into your yard. How will you deal with your Wolfhound's hurting a neighbor's pet?

Tie-outs and trolleys are also totally unacceptable for a Wolfhound, or for any dog. There are too many opportunities for a dog to get tangled with these devices. If you can't have a good-sized, sturdy fence, you shouldn't have a Wolfhound.

Children

Irish Wolfhounds are generally good with children. But common sense must be used with active puppies and young dogs around small children. A puppy can knock down a child in play. Therefore, your Wolfhound should be monitored when with young children to make sure that no one is hurt.

You are responsible for ensuring that children treat the dog properly. No dog wants to be pounced on or pestered when sleeping or in her crate. The dog may not always welcome hugging or clinging by a child if she is not accustomed to such behavior. Teach the child how to pet the dog gently while talking to her. Don't allow children to annoy the dog or play with her ears or tail. Closely watch your dog's reactions to unfamiliar children who may be more assertive or enthusiastic than she is comfortable with.

Even though your Wolfhound is big, she is not structurally built to be ridden; don't put a child on her back. She is also not a draft dog suited to pulling a cart, so that too is not an advisable activity.

Remember that an Irish Wolfhound puppy will soon weigh more, much more, than a young child.

Other Pets

Irish Wolfhounds enjoy the company of other nonaggressive dogs, especially other sighthounds. If you have the inclination and resources, one of the nicest things you can get for your Wolfhound is another Wolfhound.

One advantage to having more than one Wolfhound is that they play with each other and therefore are less dependent on you for entertainment. Get each one at different times so you can focus on bonding and training one at a time. Younger dogs tend to respect their elders and learn from them. When you get the second dog, the older dog will help train the newcomer, showing her the ways of the household. This is especially helpful with housebreaking.

If you have another dog when you bring home your Wolfhound, give your current dog a lot of extra attention so she knows that she is still senior to the new dog in rank and in your affection. Pet the current dog first; feed her first; give her treats first; let her out first.

TIP

The Perils of Overheating

When you take a dog with you, remember not to leave her alone in a car when the weather is warm, even with the windows cracked. The temperature in the car will get very high very fast. Dogs don't have efficient cooling systems. In even ten minutes, you could return to a very sick dog, or worse.

Introduce them on neutral territory and on lead. Don't let them out in the yard alone together until you know they are comfortable with each other. If there is a big size difference, as with an adult and a puppy, monitor their play to make sure the puppy isn't hurt.

If you already have a Wolfhound who has a tendency to chase smaller animals, you may not want to add a small dog, cat, or similarly

sized pet to your household. Your Wolfhound may consider the small dog a toy or an animal to chase, resulting in possible injury or worse.

Other Animals

Remember that the Irish Wolfhound was bred for centuries to chase, hunt, and bring down game. Therefore, assume that small animals may be chased and possibly hurt.

Some Wolfhounds are fine with cats, especially if they are raised with them. Others are not. You must evaluate each Wolfhound on an individual basis. If you already have a cat when you bring home your Wolfhound, introduce them indoors with the dog on leash and under control, with the cat having freedom to leave. Pet the cat to show the hound that the cat is a member of the family.

Most Wolfhounds will consider rabbits and similar animals as their natural prey. Outdoors, all small animals may be considered fair game, including yours. If your neighborhood has free-roaming pets, forewarn your neighbors. Your Wolfhound may well chase strange animals that enter her fenced yard.

If you have a horse, teach your Wolfhound as a puppy to respect the horse. Do not assume that the hound will not chase the horse. Making this assumption can result in serious injury to the dog.

Socialization

Some Irish Wolfhounds are extroverts; others are introverts. This is partly their individual temperament, but part is the result of the

Wolfhounds enjoy the company of most other dogs, whatever their size.

Your Wolfhound will enjoy going with you whenever possible.

dogs' experiences, especially as puppies. You can make a big positive difference by socializing your puppy.

The purpose of socializing is to produce a happy, well-adjusted, confident dog that finds the world a friendly place. For a young puppy, almost everything is new. It is a good time to expose her to as many new people, places, animals, and things as you can, when she is most receptive. The more she experiences as a youngster, the more comfortable she will be with new experiences for the rest of her life.

When you have people come to your house, if they are agreeable, have them meet your Wolfhound. Take her for walks in the neighborhood, always on lead, and introduce her to your neighbors and their children. Go for walks in area parks. Take her anywhere you can where dogs are welcome.

When you go on a trip and stay at a place that allows dogs, take your Wolfhound. If you think you might use a pet sitter in the future, arrange for a friend whom your Wolfhound knows to come to your home when you aren't there, to feed her and let her out in the yard.

One never knows when a dog may need to stay in a kennel. If your Wolfhound's first experience being kenneled is when she is older,

Be it ever so humble, there is no place like home for relaxing.

she may well be stressed, even to the point of refusing food or getting sick. To avoid the stress, give her the experience when she is young. Find an area kennel that is acceptable and let her stay there for a day or overnight a few times. Make sure the kennel is sized for and equipped to handle a giant dog. She needs to have an individual run and not be crated. Make sure it is a positive experience so that she has a good time and learns that you will come get her shortly.

Many obedience clubs and some pet supply stores offer puppy kindergarten classes that are excellent places for your Wolfhound to meet other people and other dogs in a new location. Gentle introductory training is offered, but the real value is the new experience it offers your puppy.

As your Wolfhound encounters new people, animals, and places, if she meets them confidently, encourage her and praise her. Make sure her behavior is appropriate; don't let her jump on people or dogs.

If she is nervous or anxious, don't coo, soothe, or pet her because that will reinforce her apprehension. Instead, act confident yourself, for you are her leader, and she will look to you for an appropriate attitude. Don't push her; let her approach at her own speed. As she meets more new people, animals, and places, and nothing bad happens, and as she sees you as confident and unafraid, she will become more assured. If she is food motivated, carry some extra special treats with you. When she

Irish Wolfhounds shine on many stages. The breed is widely sought out for celebrations of Celtic heritage and makes a grand addition to the fun.

If you don't teach your Wolfhound good manners, she won't be welcome when company visits.

meets a new person, slip your acquaintance a couple of treats, if he is willing, to feed your Wolfhound. Your Wolfhound will learn that new people are wonderful and a source of goodies.

Basic Training

Irish Wolfhounds are very strong dogs. Decide what you want her to be able to do, and if possible, begin her training as a puppy when she is smaller. Many Wolfhounds are given to rescue organizations because the owners cannot control them; make sure that doesn't happen with your dog.

You don't have to teach her everything in the standard obedience book, although you can. Pick and choose the behaviors you will find useful. Some good Wolfhound behaviors include

✔ Walk on a lead without pulling
✔ Come when called
✔ Wait (don't go through a door until you say "Okay")
✔ Sit—only because it is easier to tell a dog to lie Down from a sitting position
✔ Down
✔ Stay

Walk on Lead Without Pulling

Even after your Wolfhound has become accustomed to a lead, she may pull. Even though you don't necessarily require her to stay in an obedience heel position at your left side, it is annoying to walk a dog that is

pulling hard. Two techniques are effective in teaching a dog not to pull.

The first technique involves your stopping when your dog pulls on the lead. Begin your walk. When the lead gets taut, stop—you turn into an immovable post. Your Wolfhound will notice that you have stopped and that pulling doesn't get you to move forward. She will turn back and look at you, which will produce some slack in the lead. When there is slack, you can start walking again. She will pull again, and

TIP

Training Goals

Be realistic in your expectations when training your Wolfhound. Remember that she is a puppy for a long time, even when she is big and appears to be grown-up.

TIP

Training Should Be Fun

Keep training sessions very short, perhaps five minutes, and have several sessions each day as part of playtime. Keep your tone positive; don't correct your Wolfhound for not doing something she hasn't learned yet. Make it fun and upbeat so that your Wolfhound will enjoy her lessons. Use treats to entice the behavior you want and to reward her.

Puppies, like children, are learning all the time. Start short, gentle lessons while your Wolfhound is quite young.

the lead will become taut again. Again, you stop. The lead is your signal. When it is taut, you stop. When it is slack, you walk. Your dog will learn that she only gets to walk when the lead is slack. Because she wants to walk, she will make sure the lead is slack. Note that the situation shows her what will work for her and what won't; you don't need to correct her.

The second technique requires more dexterity on your part. You must do more than just stop; you must be able to turn around and walk in the opposite direction. This teaches your dog not just not to pull, but also to pay attention to where you are and where you are going.

Ready? Start your walk. As your Wolfhound walks ahead, paying no attention to you and before the lead is tight, make an about turn and stride off firmly in the other direction. The remaining slack in the lead will become taut and will jerk the dog in the direction you are now walking. Note: Don't jerk so hard that you might hurt her. Your dog will be startled at the change of direction, but she will adjust and head with you in the new direction. As she forges ahead again, about to pull, but before the lead becomes taut, turn around and go quickly in the opposite direction. Again she will be jerked to go along with you. Note again that you are not correcting her; the situation is. She did not pay attention and did not see your change of direction. After a few about-turns, she will keep much closer to you so she doesn't miss the change of direction again. No siree; she won't be fooled again!

Your goal is pleasant walks, with you walking the dog rather than the other way around. When your Wolfhound forgets her manners, a few posts and about-turns incorporated into your walk will remind her.

Although he may want to, don't let a child too small to control your Wolfhound walk her. It is too easy for the lead to slip from a child's hands, and then the dog is gone.

Come When Called

Come when called must start as soon as you get your puppy. Call her name and the command **Come**. Encourage her to come with your voice. Squat or bend down with your arms open to welcome her. When she comes, pet her, love her, praise her. Let her know she is most wonderful for coming to you. Carry some treats in your pockets. Several times each day and evening, call her to you and give her a treat. She will learn that it is always wonderful and rewarding to come to you.

To ensure that she always feels this way, you must never ever call your Wolfhound to you to do something she won't like. Don't call her to you to get a pill, get a bath, be groomed, or to participate in any other process she doesn't like. If you do, you are teaching her NOT to come when you call.

Don't expect any sighthound to come when called when she is in the middle of a chase. She is much too focused on what she is chasing to hear you. But if she ever gets loose and you call her in the first couple of seconds, she may well respond, and you can avoid the possible disaster of her running away.

Wait

It is very annoying for your giant dog to exit the car before you are ready or to push ahead of you through a door. So, teach her to **Wait** until you say "Okay." Open the door just far enough so that you can block her exit, and then say "Wait." Don't let her push through,

Always take the special nature of sighthound temperament into account when obedience training your Wolfhound.

Teach your Wolfhound to sit by putting her in the sit position using the tuck method.

and hold her if necessary. Repeat the command as needed. When she isn't pushing and all is under control, release her with "Okay," and let her through the door.

TIP

Wolfhounds Are "Softies"

Wolfhounds are extremely sensitive and react negatively to harsh corrections. When training, focus on positive reinforcement, including treats, praise, and petting, with minimal use of harsh corrections and harsh vocal commands.

Sit

Sitting is not a position that Wolfhounds do often on their own. They tend to either stand or lie down. But because it is easiest to instruct a dog to lie down from the sitting position, it is useful to teach a dog the **Sit** command.

Usually, one teaches a dog to sit by saying "Sit" and then putting the dog in the Sit position. This is true for Wolfhounds, too, except for the method of putting the dog in the Sit position. Hold your dog's collar with one hand and with your other arm, tuck her into a sitting position. This is done by running your arm over the back of her rear legs and then pushing with your arm on the back of both her knees.

Down

Down is a very useful command for a Wolfhound to know, whether she is blocking the television or you have company not familiar with a giant dog.

Put her in the Sit position. Hold an extra tasty treat (a bit of meat or cheese) in front of her nose. Lower it at an angle toward the floor, so that the dog follows it with her muzzle; she will end up lying down. Say "Down" as you lower the treat to the floor. When her elbows have hit the floor, assuming her rear is still down, tell her what a good dog she is and give her the treat.

Stay

Even though the **Stay** command is not critical, it is a great way to impress you friends. The Stay command tells the dog to remain in the position she is currently in until you release her. The most useful position to use with Stay is the dog lying down.

*To teach the **Down** command, have your Wolfhound sitting and use a tasty treat to ease her into the desired position.*

The secret of the Stay command is to progress in very small increments. Have the Wolfhound on lead and put her in the Down position. Stand on the lead as close to the dog as you can to help prevent her from getting up. Say "Stay," and put your right hand in front of her face, open palm facing the dog. Count to five, release her by saying "Okay" and praise her. When she will stay for a count of five, count to ten. If she gets up, start over. Little by little, increase your count. Practice standing at her side; then practice standing right in front of her. When she has the concept, take a step back. Little by little, she will stay longer and longer. Remember to release her, though, unless she falls asleep.

Dealing with Problems

The best way to deal with bad habits is to avoid them: Don't let bad habits get started, and don't let the dog have the opportunity to be bad. You must monitor her closely as a puppy. You must think ahead and not give her the chance to misbehave. You won't avoid all problems, but you can certainly keep them to a minimum.

Chewing

Puppies chew. They chew when they are teething, investigating something new, playing, or bored. Give her something she is allowed to chew, making sure she cannot swallow it or chew off a piece she might swallow. Keep her away from items you don't want her to chew.

This can be done by crating or confining her when you cannot watch her and by supervising her behavior when you can. Correct her if she puts her mouth on something you don't want her to chew. If you can prevent her chewing the furniture, books, shoes, walls, and more as a puppy, she will be much less likely to do it as an adult.

There are products you can spray on objects that your puppy might chew to deter the chewing. In addition to them, you might spray

TIP

Wolfhound Versus Tiger

Few things are safe to give a Wolfhound to chew. A toy manufacturer gave a new ball to a zoo to see if it would endure the abuse of a Bengal tiger. The ball fared very well. When given to a Wolfhound, it was destroyed.

Rawhide bones, even very large ones, aren't recommended for Wolfhounds that can chew off pieces and swallow them before you can intervene.

on a deodorant that contains alum; it tastes bad and prevents chewing.

Digging

Dogs dig. It is fun; it is part of their nature. Even though Wolfhounds don't have digging as part of their original function as some breeds do, when they do dig, they produce a very big hole. The best way to prevent digging is not to give the dog the opportunity. Either have someone with her outside, or when she stops running, invite her back inside. Your Wolfhound doesn't need hours in the yard. She will get bored and find something to do, and you may not approve of what she does. If your puppy manages to dig a hole anyway, you might try putting some of her stool in it and then filling it up with the dirt. That should prevent her digging in that hole. Of course, she can always dig in another place.

Running Away

Wolfhounds were bred to run, chase, and hunt. You are not going to train the instinct out of them. Therefore, you must make sure your Wolfhound doesn't have the opportunity by keeping her on lead and making sure your backyard fence is secure.

For insurance, microchip your dog as soon as you get her. If she does run away and is found, she can be identified and returned to you.

Irish Wolfhounds enjoy romping outdoors; but if they become bored or get adventurous, they may entertain themselves by digging.

A four-month-old Irish Wolfhound will be larger than adults of many other breeds.

Further, make sure you teach her to Come when called. If she gets loose and you call her immediately, she may well respond, and you can catch her before she goes.

Network

The problems discussed in this chapter are problems dealt with by all dog owners. Irish Wolfhounds just put their unique flavor on the situations. Many problems other dogs cause—barking, high energy, housebreaking—are not problems with Wolfhounds. Keep in touch with your breeder and other Wolfhounders. You can share helpful hints, solutions, and stories and enjoy being part of the large Irish Wolfhound community. With your good planning, common sense, and networking with others, your Wolfhound can fulfill her potential to be a much-loved member of your family and a credit to her illustrious heritage.

ACTIVITIES WITH YOUR WOLFHOUND

If you and your Wolfhound are inclined to get off the couch, you can enjoy many competitive and athletic events that not only highlight your dog's strengths and strengthen your bond but that are fun, too. Most of these events are offered by AKC clubs. In order to participate in AKC activities, your Wolfhound must be registered with the American Kennel Club.

AKC Registration

If you get your Wolfhound from a breeder, you should get the AKC registration application from her. When this form is sent to the AKC, it will register your Wolfhound.

If your Wolfhound is already registered, you should get his AKC registration certificate. On the reverse side is a form to transfer the dog to you, the new owner. When it is completed and signed, you can send the form to AKC to record you as the Wolfhound's owner.

If your purebred Irish Wolfhound is not registered or the AKC papers are not available and

Many obedience clubs offer Canine Good Citizen (CGC) tests following some of their regularly scheduled obedience classes.

you want to participate in AKC activities, you can get an Indefinite Listing Privilege (ILP) number. The ILP registration allows your Wolfhound to participate in AKC companion and performance events, such as obedience, agility, and lure coursing. Details on applying for an ILP number is on the AKC's web site, *www.akc.org.*

Canine Good Citizen

The Canine Good Citizen (CGC) program is intended to reward dogs who have good manners at home and in the community. A minimum of obedience training and socialization should enable your Wolfhound to earn the CGC title.

Owners of Irish Wolfhounds will find the bond with their dogs enhanced through participation in competitive activities.

Your Wolfhound will be tested on the following behaviors:

✔ Acceptance of a friendly stranger

✔ Ability to sit politely for petting

✔ Appearance and grooming, which includes letting a stranger gently brush or comb him

✔ Ability to walk on a loose lead

✔ Ability to walk through a crowd

✔ Sit and Down on command and Stay in place

✔ Come when called

✔ Reaction to another dog

✔ Reaction to distraction

✔ Supervised separation, where someone else holds your Wolfhound's lead while you go out of sight for three minutes

Obedience

If you and your dog enjoy training, you can earn AKC obedience titles. With the current training techniques emphasizing positive reinforcement, more Irish Wolfhounds are competing in the obedience ring. Some breeds and some Irish Wolfhounds take to obedience tasks easily. Others do not. So be guided by your own dog's preferences in deciding how much you want to do. Some Wolfhounds don't find sitting comfortable, have a minimum work ethic, and have low energy. Wolfhounds with these tendencies are unlikely to be obedience stars. But, if you both like it, there are three titles you can aim for. Your dog doesn't need to be a star to get a title; a passing score will do fine.

Companion Dog (CD)

The CD title can be earned from the Novice level class in obedience trials. The Novice exercises are heeling (on and off lead), stand for examination, recall, one-minute sit (and stay),

Tired of lying around? There are many activities you can enjoy with your Wolfhound.

and three-minute down (and stay). All but the sit and down are done with just you and your Wolfhound; the long sit and long down are done with groups of other dogs.

Companion Dog Excellent (CDX)

The CDX title is the goal when competing in Open classes. The Open exercises are all done off lead. They are heeling, drop on recall,

The Irish Wolfhounds on the left and right enjoy their obedience class with an Italian Greyhound and a Scottish Deerhound.

Swimming is great exercise, with no trauma to bones and joints.

retrieve, retrieve over a high jump, broad jump, long sit (three minutes), and long down (five minutes).

Utility Dog (UD)

Utility-level dogs compete for a UD degree. The Utility exercises include heeling using hand signals only, scent discrimination where your dog retrieves an item you touched, directed retrieve of a glove you point to, and directed jumping over the jump you indicate. Like Open, all Utility exercises are done off lead.

Classes offered by obedience clubs are the best places to train your dog and see how far you both want to go. It is important to train with a class rather than only at home because your dog has to perform the obedience exercises with other dogs and distractions. Even though you will practice at home, if your dog performs only at home, his training is definitely incomplete.

The instructors are usually obedience club members who compete with their own dogs. Most of the instructors work with dog breeds that have a great aptitude for obedience. Try to find an instructor who has had experience working with sighthounds, giant dogs, or other nontraditional obedience breeds and who supports your efforts. Ask others who compete with unusual dogs in obedience in your area what trainers they would recommend. It may take some hunting, but the result might be a joyful experience with a multititled dog.

Lure Coursing

Lure coursing is an event where your Irish Wolfhound can shine. It simulates what the

Lure coursing gives Irish Wolfhounds the opportunity to run and chase.

breed was created to do: chase game. The dogs chase an artificial lure, which is actually a white plastic garbage bag, that appears to race around the course, running in a zigzag fashion, much as a rabbit would race around a field. The length of the course the dogs run is approximately 800–900 yards (720–810 m).

Lure coursing trials are held under the auspices of both the AKC and the American Sighthound Field Association. Your dog is evaluated on how well he runs the course, chasing the "bunny." It is not just the fastest dog who wins. The dogs are also rated on enthusiasm, ability to follow the lure, agility, and endurance.

In lure coursing, usually two or three dogs of the same breed are run together on the course. Your Wolfhound will run only with other Wolfhounds and only with those who are at the same level of the competition.

If you plan to lure course with your Wolfhound, seek a breeder whose dogs participate

successfully in the sport. Getting a puppy from a line that excels in competitive running increases your chances of getting a Wolfhound who will do well. Additionally, you will have a lure coursing mentor in your breeder. (See HOW-TO: Lure Coursing Training, page 90).

The eagerness of this Wolfhound to start his run is evidence of his enjoyment of lure coursing.

The exhibitor "sets up" or poses his dog, hoping the judge will select it as best. The scene is the Hound Group competition at the annual Westminster Kennel Club dog show.

Titles

The ASFA titles your dog can earn are its Field Championship (FCh) title and its Lure Courser of Merit (LCM) title. AKC offers noncompetitive lure coursing tests to determine your Wolfhound's coursing instinct; if this is passed, the hound has a Junior Courser (JC) title. AKC titles Senior Courser (SC) and Master Courser (MC) are achieved by earning qualifying scores run with other dogs. AKC titles Field Championship (FC), and Lure Courser Excellent (LCX) are won by earning championship points.

Dog Shows

At dog shows, your dog competes with other Wolfhounds to earn his conformation champi-onship. The judge evaluates the dogs on how close they are to the perfect Wolfhound as described by the Irish Wolfhound standard. He looks at the dogs standing and trotting and examines each with his hands. He selects the best quality male and female who are not already champions to get points toward their championship. A dog can earn from zero to five points at a show, depending on how many other Wolfhounds he defeats. To earn his championship, your Wolfhound must earn 15 points under at least three different judges, and at least two of the wins must be worth three points or more.

If you would like your dog to earn his championship, select a breeder whose dogs have earned their championships. Tell your breeder that you are interested in a show potential puppy and that you will show the dog. The breeder will help you select a puppy that will most likely be competitive at dog shows. She can teach you how to groom your dog for the show ring and guide you in learning about dog shows.

Training for dog shows is simpler than training for obedience or performance competitions. Socialization is again important because your Wolfhound will be around new people, places, and other dogs. Your Wolfhound must stand and accept the judge going over his entire body, including looking at his teeth. Practice having people go over your dog as a judge would so he will become accustomed to the procedure. Teach your dog to trot at a moderate speed in a straight line by your side, which the judge will ask you to do to evaluate his soundness.

Many people, when showing their dogs, use bait to make the dog stand at attention and look alert. The bait is a special treat that your dog particularly favors. Because your dog will be standing when shown, don't train him to sit for treats, or you will find him sitting when you show him the bait in the show ring. Instead, when you give him the treat at home, have him stand, and maybe stretch just a little to get the treat.

Look on AKC's web site to locate dog clubs that put on dog shows in your area. Some of them may hold handling classes where you can learn how to handle your Wolfhound. Many clubs also hold matches, which are practice dog shows. Matches are excellent events at which to practice with your Wolfhound before entering an actual show.

The judge will have the exhibitors trot their Wolfhounds around the ring as a group to help him decide which is best.

TIP

Wolfhound Intelligence

If your Wolfhound does not excel in obedience, it does not mean he is not intelligent. Although all AKC breeds can compete, the obedience exercises best suit high-energy dogs whose functions involve frequent owner commands and close focus on their owner, such as sporting and herding breeds. Wolfhounds were developed to chase and bring down game. They work independently at a distance from their owners, make their own decisions, and focus intently to get the job done. Criticizing a sighthound for poor performance in obedience is like criticizing a German mathematics expert for poor performance in a fine arts test in French.

This well-mannered Wolfhound is welcomed as a therapy dog and as part of a pet care program for elementary school children.

Agility

Agility is one of the most popular and fast growing AKC events. At agility trials, dogs race around a timed obstacle course, demonstrating their agility and versatility. The goal is to run the course within the standard time and with the fewest faults. The obstacles include

✔ the A-frame, which the dog must go over

✔ the dog walk, an elevated board that the dog must walk across

✔ the seesaw, on which the dog walks up one side and down the other

✔ the pause table, where the dog must get on and stay for a short time

✔ a variety of jumps

✔ the weave poles, which the dog must go around alternately, weaving in and out

✔ tunnels and a closed chute, which is a tunnel made of fabric, which the dog must go through

There are three levels of competition: Novice, Open, and Excellent. They differ in the number of obstacles on the course and the amount of handling or teamwork expected between you and your dog. The courses can also vary with the obstacles included. The Standard course may include all the obstacles, while Jumpers with Weaves excludes the contact obstacles, those where the dog must touch a certain part of the obstacle. Preferred classes are offered with slightly lower jump heights and longer standard times.

If your dog gets a qualifying score, he earns a "leg" toward his title. There are many titles in agility, based on the combination of level, the type of course, and whether it is preferred or not.

Although agility is open to all AKC breeds, the obstacles don't change size for the different breeds other than varying the height of the jumps. The dog walk is made of wood 12 inches (30 cm) wide, which must look different to a Chihuahua than it would to a Wolfhound. The biggest potential obstacle is the open or closed tunnel, which is no more than 24 inches (61 cm) high. A dog can crouch going through a tunnel. But at some height, a Wolfhound will just be too tall to compete. You can do agility with a petite Wolfhound, but the big boys (and girls) just won't get through the tunnels. If you are dedicated to both agility and an Irish Wolfhound, a small female is most likely to be successful.

A dog's sense of smell is estimated to be 10,000 times that of a human's, so tracking should be easy for your dog.

Tracking

Even though sighthounds hunt by sight, as dogs, Irish Wolfhounds have powerful noses that they can use to earn a tracking title. Tracking is AKC's version of competitive search and rescue, where the dogs show their ability to follow a human scent. Unlike other competitions, a dog needs to qualify only once to earn each of the three tracking titles.

The first-level tracking title is TD for Tracking Dog. The second level, TDX, for Tracking Dog Excellent, has the dog follow a longer, older track. Variable Surface Tracking (VST) has the dog follow a track which goes across different surfaces, perhaps across pavement or through a building. A dog that has completed all three tracking titles can also claim the title Champion Tracker (CT).

Training for tracking uses lots of treats. In the grass, you or a friend lays a short track, maybe 6 feet (2 m) long, by shuffling your feet as you walk. Put a few treats along the track and at the end. With your dog on lead, start him at the beginning by pointing your finger on the ground where the track commences and encourage him to smell. Encourage him to follow the track to get the treat, then praise him greatly for doing so. Slowly, make the track longer. Eventually, add some moderate turns. Once he gets the concept of using his nose, your Wolfhound will be tracking.

Junior Showmanship

If you have children in your family who are between 9 and 17 years old and who are interested in dog shows, they might want to investigate Junior Showmanship (JS). Junior Showmanship is a competition held at most dog shows wherein the youngsters compete with their dogs and are judged solely on their handling ability.

JS is divided into classes based on age and experience. Novice classes are for less experienced handlers. The Open classes are for those more experienced. Both Novice and Open are further divided by age into Junior, Intermediate, and Senior classes.

JS is a great opportunity for youngsters to improve their handling skills, learn good sportsmanship, make new friends, and have fun with the family Wolfhound.

HOW-TO: LURE COURSING

Socialization

To train your Wolfhound for lure coursing, begin by socializing him extensively, so he will be confident and comfortable with other people, places, and dogs. He needs this experience and attitude to be able to focus on the lure and not be distracted. Attend puppy kindergarten classes where he can play with other puppies. Let friends take him for a walk. The period between 12 and 16 weeks is an especially important time during which your puppy needs to develop his social skills.

Puppy Training

When he is a young puppy, starting at about 10 weeks,

get him interested in a lure by using a pole about 6 feet (2 m) long (or longer) with a 6-foot (2-m) (or longer) length of string attached to one end. Attach a bit of fur, fleece, or a toy on the end of the string. Drag and bounce the lure around on the ground, encouraging your dog to try to catch it. Tease him with the lure when he's on one side of the fence and the lure on the other. Let him catch it occasionally. Don't tire the puppy; always leave him wanting more.

Initial Training on a Course

Contact a lure coursing club (you can find them on the AKC's web site) and find out when they have practice. Very

young hounds (younger than four months) should not be allowed to run a lure course. Remember these puppies are growing rapidly and are susceptible to injury. Still, it is great for socializing, and your youngster can watch other hounds practicing. Young dogs do learn from watching older dogs perform. Don't discourage him from barking or pulling toward the lure.

A six-month or older puppy may be allowed to run a short course, perhaps 100 feet (30 m), but only in a straight line and only in one direction. As he grows, you can lengthen the distance, but keep it straight and in one direction. At this point, have him run by himself, not with other dogs. Don't tire the puppy; keep it fun.

When your Wolfhound is learning, ask the lure operator for slow jerky starts. Let your puppy catch the lure at the end of the straight run.

More Practice on a Course

As he approaches a year old, you can lengthen the course and introduce a shallow, not sharp, turn to the course. Your puppy's bones are still developing, and sharp turns can cause permanent

Your dog is held with a slip lead until you are signaled to release him.

While you guide him, your Wolfhound's instincts as a sighthound enable him to lure course.

damage. At this point, you can consider letting your Wolfhound run with another. The Wolfhound he runs with should be experienced and clean-running. He will be allowed to run with others only when he will focus on the lure and not play with the other dogs.

Conditioning

If you lure course your Wolfhound, keep him in condition to run. Watch his weight. Let him have the opportunity to run frequently in a fenced enclosure. As he matures, long walks are suitable. Wolfhounds need a great deal of exer-cise to be fit to compete. Like any athlete, he will have more fun, more success, and less injury if he is in shape for the sport.

Equipment

The equipment you need to participate in lure coursing is simple. You need three blankets, in yellow, pink, and blue, one of which is worn by your dog to identify him during the run. Many clubs have these in various sizes that you may borrow, or you can make your own. You also need a slip lead, which is used to hold your dog until signaled to run, and then to release him instantly. Remember to bring your own water to practice sessions and trials, for these may not be available. Bring a first aid kit, too, just in case.

INFORMATION

Organizations
American Kennel Club
5580 Centerview Drive
Raleigh, NC 27606-3390
919-233-9767
Web site: *www.akc.org*

Irish Wolfhound Club of America
President: Randy Valenti
6904 Pull Tight Hill Road
College Grove, TN 37046
615-599-4665

Secretary: Judy Simon
7155 County Road 26
Maple Plain, MN 55359
763-479-1638
Web site: *www.iwclubofamerica.org*

Note: Officers and contacts will change. Please check the IWCA web site. You can also check with the AKC to find the current contacts for the IWCA.

American Sighthound Field Association
Secretary: Russ Jacobs
7045 SE 61st Street
Tecumseh, KS 66542
785-379-5430
corressecy@asfa.org
Web site: *www.asfa.org*
Note: Officers change. Please check the ASFA web site.

The Irish Wolfhound Club of Canada
Web site: *www.iwcc.ca*

The Irish Wolfhound Club (United Kingdom)
Web site: *www.theirishwolfhoundclub.org*

Irish Wolfhound Club of Ireland
Web site: *http://homepage.eircom.net*

Magazines
Harp and Hound
The official publication of the IWCA and available to members. Contact the IWCA for membership information.

AKC Gazette
General dog and multi-breed magazine. Contact the AKC for subscription information.

Regardless of their rugged, outdoor heritage, Irish Wolfhounds are genuine companion dogs and want most to be with their favorite people.

With regular grooming, an Irish Wolfhound is relatively easy to keep clean and makes a very agreeable house dog.

Books

Donovan, John A. K. *The Irish Wolfhound: Great Symbol of Ireland.* Loveland, CO: Alpine Publications, 1986.

Gordon, John F. *The Irish Wolfhound.* New York, NY: Arco Publishing Company, Inc., 1977.

McBryde, Mary. *The Irish Wolfhound, Symbol of Celtic Splendor.* New York, NY: Howell Books, 1998.

Samaha, Joel. *The New Complete Irish Wolfhound.* New York, NY: Howell Books, 1991.

About the Author

Nikki Riggsbee is an AKC judge of Irish Wolfhounds, plus all other AKC hound and working breeds and some sporting breeds. She breeds, shows, and lives with another giant breed, Great Danes, which were used in re-creating the Irish Wolfhound from the edge of extinction. She knows firsthand the challenges and joys of a giant breed and mentors new owners on living with giant dogs. She has been published in several dog magazines, written a booklet on Great Danes, and has presented numerous seminars on evaluating dogs.

Acknowledgments

Sincere thanks to the many Irish Wolfhound owners who shared their knowledge and stories of their breed, especially Anne Gallant and Gretchen Bernardi, both of whom are Wolfhound breeder-judges, who provided feedback on each chapter. Appreciation to Dr. Pam Hendrickson (a Wolfhound breeder as well) and Dr. Beverly Brimacomb for reviewing the health topics. And much gratitude to Seymour Weiss, editor and knowledgeable dog person, for the invaluable help, guidance, and suggestions he provided for this book.

Important Note

This pet owner's manual tells the reader how to buy or adopt, and care for an Irish Wolfhound. The author and publisher consider it important to point out that the advice given in the book is meant primarily for normally developed dogs of excellent physical health and sound temperament.

Anyone who acquires a fully-grown dog should be aware that the animal has already formed its basic impressions of human beings. The new owner should observe the animal carefully, including its behavior toward humans, and, whenever possible, should meet the previous owner.

Caution is further advised in the association of children with dogs, and in meeting with other dogs, and in exercising the dog without a leash.

These matters assume greater-than-normal importance when the dog is of a giant breed.

Even well-behaved and carefully supervised dogs can sometimes damage property or cause accidents. It is therefore in the owner's interest to be adequately insured against such eventualities, and we strongly urge all dog owners to purchase a liability policy that also covers their dog.

Photo Credits

Cheryl Ertelt: 4, 7, 10, 11, 14 (top), 19, 21, 22, 24, 31, 35, 37, 39, 40, 43, 45, 48, 49 (top and bottom), 56, 61, 62, 67, 73, 74, 77, 78, 79, 83 (bottom), 84, 87, 92; Kent Dannen: 2, 5, 9, 12, 13, 14 (bottom), 15, 16, 23, 25, 26, 30, 33, 36, 38, 41, 42, 44, 55, 57, 58, 60, 64, 65, 66, 70, 71, 72 (bottom), 75, 81, 82, 85, 88; Michele Earle-Bridges: 18, 78 (top); Tara Darling: 50, 54, 72 (top), 80, 83 (top), 84, 86, 93.

Cover Photos

Front cover: Kent Dannen; inside front cover: Cheryl Ertelt; inside back cover: Tara Darling; back cover: Tara Darling.

All inquiries should be addressed to:
Barron's Educational Series, Inc.
250 Wireless Boulevard
Hauppauge, NY 11788
www.barronseduc.com

International Standard Book No. 0-7641-3027-7
Library of Congress Catalog Card No. 2004063115

Library of Congress Cataloging-in-Publication Data
Riggsbee, Nikki.
  Irish wolfhounds : everything about purchase, care, nutrition, behavior and training / Nikki Riggsbee ; illustrations by Michele Earle-Bridges.
    p. cm.
  Includes bibliographical references and index.
  ISBN 0-7641-3027-7
  1. Irish wolfhound. I. Title.

SF429.I85R54   2005
636.753'5–dc22   2004063115

Printed in China
9 8 7 6 5 4 3 2 1